Praise for *Happy*
by Alex Lemon

"One of our time's most compelling memoirs . . . An electrifying portrait of a body in crisis, and the way the soul is inexorably, reluctantly dragged along. [Lemon] has staked out his own frontier—the land of the ridiculous sublime, a country that is at the same time both wildly playful and deeply felt."

—*Esquire*

"This one is something special. . . . This is the story of a boy and his mother, but one whose tenderness sneaks up on you while you're distracted by all the blood and booze and hollering. The two of them can talk about nearly anything, but don't always have to. What Lemon and his mom have is that rarest of things in a trauma memoir, a parent-child relationship that is more than merely 'functional.' It's funkily, goofily, supremely life-affirming. Make that lifesaving."

—Laura Miller, *Salon*

"Lemon can be both Prospero and Caliban—applying luminous magic to his own dark materials, the result a dappled mixture of the two."

—*Poets & Writers Magazine*

"Dazzling . . . An unnervingly intimate, relentlessly poetic recounting of debauchery, trauma and healing. Alex Lemon's memoir is cut from the same cloth as David Carr's *The Night of the Gun* or James Frey's discredited *A Million Little Pieces*.

But whereas those autobiographies reveled in the seamy details accompanying the wild life, *Happy* is far more concerned with the party's aftermath. . . . There are few modern works that so elegantly capture a mind and, by extension, a life on the verge of disintegration."

—*Fort Worth Star-Telegram*

"Alex Lemon makes *Happy* harrowing and upbeat, writing with a poet's touch about the illness that overtook his jock life. . . . Nonfiction writers and poets have a secret alliance—working toward defining a truth instead of making it up. So when we get a twofer of a poet writing memoir, the results trend toward glinting precision."

—Karen Schechner, *The Plain Dealer*

The Daily Beast named *Happy* one of the ten best books of January 2010.

"Until he suffered a stroke his freshman year at college, Alex Lemon was a hard-partying, popular college student. He sought solace in drink and drugs before his mother stepped in to nurse him. All of this is recounted with surprising humor in this memoir about one man's struggle to overcome the unexpected."

—*The Daily Beast*

"Lemon is a compelling and inventive writer. . . . Since we know the ending (he lives to write his memoir, after all), it's a credit to Lemon's storytelling ability that he keeps readers engaged to the end."

—The Associated Press

"*Happy* is graphically raw and in-your-face: Lemon's dexterity with words forces the reader into gritty latitudes no one would visit voluntarily, and the level of detail will cause some readers to squirm. But *Happy* is an honest voyage into Lemon's keen mind, remarkable spirit and loving heart, and it shouldn't be missed."

—*Minneapolis Star Tribune*

"Poet Lemon packs the poignant wallop of a sprawling Dickensian novel with his taut, speedy memoir."

—*The Denver Post*

"A short, fast, punchy read."

—*The Oregonian*

"If you've given up on memoir—and you wouldn't be blamed for doing so, especially when it's another personal-salvation story by a formerly drug-addicted Minnesotan—you've missed Alex Lemon's *Happy*, a book that may actually redeem the genre."

—*Metro Magazine* (Minneapolis–St. Paul)

"This is one of those autobiographies that feel like a novel. This is the absolutely compelling account of the years leading up to the surgery and the healing period afterward, written in a flamboyant, comic-book style with a cast of characters who might have migrated over from a Bret Easton Ellis novel. On the other hand, the book's perceptive exploration of its author's mental degradation may remind some readers of Mark Vonnegut's chronicle of his own schizophrenia, *The Eden Express* (1975)."

—*Booklist*

"By turns harrowing and hopeful . . . *Happy* takes readers rushing along. . . . Yet even with its fascinating story of a young man battling outsized enemies, it is *Happy*'s language that truly sets it apart. Lemon shies from nothing, which can make for grueling (and graphic) reading, especially given the gravity of his subject matter. But he never uses his difficult topic for shock value; instead, thanks to his considerable poetic gifts, it becomes an avenue for exploring the human experience at its most dire."

—Eliza McGraw, *BookPage*

"A serious chronicle of unimaginable medical horrors and the heavy shit young people break through to become adults. But Lemon has also produced a page-turner on par with the best thrillers, a drop down a rabbit hole to the white liberal arts college scene and its hip-hop-referencing children. . . . Lemon's exquisite prose blasts us out of our own time, heart, brain, and body into his, making an acute empathy possible. Read this and weep, laugh, weep."

—Heather McCormack, *Library Journal* (Editors' Pick)

"The pyrotechnic prose of Alex Lemon's memoir creates an electrifying portrait of a body in crisis, and the way the soul is inexorably, reluctantly, dragged along. By the last mesmerizing page it is not merely the limits of the body that have been revealed, but a deeper truth—how becoming a man can sometimes mean holding the mother, who has been pushed away, ever closer. If ever a book was written in blood, it is this one."

—Nick Flynn, author of *Another Bullshit Night in Suck City*

"Good memoirs, however, like *Happy*, qualify as Art-with-a-capital-A. The narrative is extremely propulsive, thanks in no small part to Lemon's lush writing style. . . . He employs evocative language that conjures up Tom Wolfe and Hunter S. Thompson but never devolves into imitation."

—*Fort Worth Weekly*

"With a gift for startling description, Alex Lemon chronicles his transformation—through the awful experience of a brain stem lesion and radical surgery—from a damaged, self-hating boy to a resilient, emotionally alive adult. He takes his reader inside the terror and strangeness of illness—and gives us, along the way, a loving portrait of a devoted, wonderfully nutty mother. Lemon is a brave, headlong writer, and he captures the life of the body with vivid and memorable intensity."

—Mark Doty, author of *Dog Years* and *Fire to Fire*

"After undergoing brain surgery to stop his strokes and internal bleeding, Lemon recounts how his artist mother pushed him to not only recover, but flourish. The author is also a poet, and his colorful prose often pinpoints the feeling of failing health in ways that are genuinely terrifying. Though this may sound like a downer, *Happy* is just as much about hope."

—Jessica Armbruster, *City Pages* (Minneapolis)

"*Happy* unfurls like gauze, revealing not a wound, but a series of intricate and beautiful scars. Alex reminds us that though we can't make it through this life unscathed, we can make it through transformed."

—Robin Romm, author of *The Mercy Papers* and *The Mother Garden*

"Empathetic, vividly rendered and impossible to put down."

—*Kirkus Reviews* (starred review)

"Lemon offers a raw and honest narration of his college life, his relationships with girlfriends and family members, especially his loving and quirky mother. He dissects his repressed inner demons and recounts his continual struggle to regain his emotional and physical health following his operation. The result is a voltaic narrative that is alternately horrifying and touching."

—*Publishers Weekly*

"Told in a crazy-fast first person voice . . . it's hard to feel like you can stand up straight after reading this curvy, energetic story. *Happy* reminds me of the scene in *Goodfellas* where Ray Liotta is being chased by the helicopter—your heart rate races, your mind is trying hard to keep up, and your knees feel like they can't hold you up anymore. It is not rare that a decent writer can take you places that affect you both physically and mentally, but *Happy* takes you on a journey that may require a seat belt."

—Bookreporter.com

"Beautifully creative, vivid and brutal. . . . Lemon's precise accounts of his symptoms are of such incredible language you get the feeling that he has more strength within than he knows."

—*The Colorado Springs Independent*

"A gritty, human portrayal of a young life sidelined by reoccurring strokes . . . Call it Lemon's stroke of genius."

—*Galleycat*

HAPPY

A Memoir

Alex Lemon

SCRIBNER

New York   London   Toronto   Sydney

SCRIBNER

A Division of Simon & Schuster, Inc.
1230 Avenue of the Americas
New York, NY 10020

The names and other identifying characteristics of some people in this book have been changed.

First Scribner paperback edition October 2010

"Get Behind the Mule" written by Tom Waits and Kathleen Brennan
© 1999 Jalma Music (ASCAP).

"Prayer" from *The Past* by Galway Kinnell. Copyright © 1985 by Galway Kinnell. Reprinted by permission of Houghton Mifflin Harcourt Publishing Company. All rights reserved.

For information about special discounts for bulk purchases,
please contact Simon & Schuster Special Sales at
1-866-506-1949 or business@simonandschuster.com.

The Simon & Schuster Speakers Bureau can bring authors to your live event. For more information or to book an event contact the Simon & Schuster Speakers Bureau at 1-866-248-3049 or visit our website at www.simonspeakers.com.

Designed by Carla Jayne Jones

Manufactured in the United States of America

1   3   5   7   9   10   8   6   4   2

Library of Congress Control Number: 2009027293

ISBN 978-1-4165-5023-5
ISBN 978-1-4165-5025-9 (pbk)
ISBN 978-1-4391-6049-7 (ebook)

For Ma

i am this morning electric.
—*Denis Johnson*

This thing of darkness, I acknowledge mine.
—*Shakespeare*, The Tempest

Happy

Prologue

March 2004, St. Paul

CHOPPITY CHOP GOES THE AXE IN THE WOOD, YOU GOTTA meet me by the fall down tree . . . Moonlight slings through the windows. The hardwood floor is ice. *A shovel of dirt upon a coffin lid . . .* Blinding, the stars are rips in the sky. *And I know they'll come lookin' for me boys. I know they'll come lookin' for me . . .* In the bathroom, I yank out the earbuds, set the iPod on the dust-caked toilet tank, and turn the faucet on. Pipes groan on and off like dogs trapped in the duplex's walls. It's four A.M. and I'm twenty-four years old. I am Frankenstein's monster. I can't remember the last time I slept through the night.

I drop a towel, stopgap it against the crack below the door so I don't wake my housemate, Jonny, and then snap the razor on. Over the sink, I squirt oil onto the blades. Rub the steel teeth with my thumb. I let the machine hum for ten minutes, then clean the gunk off with a T-shirt. My brain swirls when I scrape my scalp with the vibrating blades, again and again until I'm dizzy, palming the mirror so I don't fall down. After I've finished the top, like I do each morning before I shave the back of my skull, I fingerpick the bloody rubble and pus off of the leaky scar. My brain surgery was over three years ago.

And then I work slow, shearing nubs of hair away for a half hour, clippering everything a second and third time, a fourth to shake it all up. A fifth to feel the buzzing, cicadas chewing through my eyes. *Just this, just this, just this.*

The apartment window fogs when I blow across the coffee mug. I trace fingers through the condensation, drawing eyes and a grinning, oblong face. While I sip, the portrait melts into Francis Bacon's screaming pope. Through the filthy glass, I watch the street below thicken with morning light. A slow brightness envelops the elms. Daybreak weaves Dayton Avenue with a rich, stirless luxury. The Volvo, the old Ford pickup, a tricycle on the sidewalk, rakes and a spade in the neighbor's overgrown yard—all of it shines.

The first time I wipe my hand through the steam I hardly notice the parked car. The window fogs again while I breathe. When I swipe again, I double take, then clean the glass with a sock that someone's nailed to the wall. On the street, a hatchback Escort blisters with orange light like its insides are on fire. A green

Happy

WELLSTONE! bumper sticker sits in the rear window. The sun hoists, and, inch by inch, the glow peels away. The backseat is down. The end is loaded with art supplies: two-by-fours and branches and doll parts, bottles of water and books, a blank canvas and a circular saw. Magazines and seed catalogues and gardening tools. I stare confused. The window glazes white as I exhale. Curled in the car seat, Ma is sleeping inside.

I

1

March 1997, Macalester College

The world whirls when I crack open. Bookshelf, poster board, the windows wink their eyes. The digital clock is a red blur. Every light pulses yelloworange and brilliant, and the TV is a blue splash.

When I stand, the dorm room spins and I tip, slamming my chin into the bed frame. My temple rocks off of the cinder-block wall and I crash back to the mattress. The first pounding breath is *Good morning you asshole* and my insides rubberband.

Woozy and flushed, I thrash through the bedcovers while the cave of my room rolls. I lip-smack away the bloody taste in my mouth. The more I struggle to focus, the more my vision twirls. I'm hazy faced. I'm fucked.

The bedsprings shriek when I slide off the mattress,

7

and planting my feet in a heap of clothes, I rise for a second, and then go facedown. I gnarl the insides of my cheeks and bite my tongue. Rolling to my back, I gulp the blood down so I don't choke.

"SHIT. SHIIIIIIIIIIIIIIIIIIT!" I yell, laughing. This is a dream; I'm the first man on Mars. "Jesus Christ, man! I'm down! MAN DOWN! Did you see that, Brad?" I look around the spinning dorm for my roommate. "I'm a fucking mess. A mess, man, a mess!" The floor is covered in moldy T-shirts and socks. "I'm like fuckin' Gumby down here." I try to slow my breath. "Hey, Brad. How 'bout a hand? Yo, Brad?"

Lying in the dust balls, I bark for help.

I try to get up again, and smash into the wooden legs of Brad's bed, and fall back down. Each time I rise a giant fist knocks the wind out of me. Sitting on my knees, my head is all clatter and thud. I rock feebly from side to side. I go facedown on the warm slick floor.

I swish bloody acid between the gaps in my teeth and swallow back a mouthful of puke. Blood-fur covers my tongue. The computer monitor quakes when I finally make it up. I cover my head with a wet towel but nothing blunts out the throbbing. Half of my face is numb.

I must have drunk a bottle of Drano last night, snorted a bag of glass, and leapt open-armed from the top of the stairs. A tree. A roof. The moon.

There is a warm beer on my desk and more in the fridge. A bunch of Vicodin in the drawer. I pop a handful of pills and chug. With my eyes half-shut, I watch students milling around outside.

"HAPPY! HURRY THE FUCK UP." THE SHAKING DOOR STARTLES me. "Happy, let's go!"

I've been staring out the window all day, watching campus beehive into spring while Sam Cooke sings the same songs over and over on my stereo. Hours ago, Brad came in and grabbed his backpack. My sketchbook was open in my lap but I hadn't drawn anything, only rubbed my hands with oil pastels and fingerprinted the paper. I grinned at him, said I wasn't going to class, that I had another sore throat, the crud, and then slapped myself. He laughed when I gave him the thumbs-up. I couldn't feel my body.

"Yo!" Someone kicks the door again, and I realize the light I've been watching clamor through the oaks has nearly vanished.

"It's time for practice, Happy!" The door jolts. "Let's go, you pussy."

"Happy. Get a move on!" It's a different voice. The doorknob turns. "Move, man! Let's go, Chet!"

My head is so fuzzy, a minute passes before I figure out they're yelling at me. I'm still not used to these new nicknames—my girlfriend and Casey and Brad are the only people who call me by my real name. Some of my teammates started calling me Chet after Chet Lemon, an outfielder who used to play for the Detroit Tigers. Everyone else, even people I don't know, calls me Happy. Happy, Happy, Happy.

"I'm going I'm going, you fuck-O's!" The words mash in my mouth. A Chet Lemon baseball card is pushpinned above my desk. I woke one morning last week, whipped my pockets inside out, and a cooked chicken breast and the Chet Lemon baseball card fell out. *Happy* was written in Sharpie up and down my arms. My hands were flayed. They looked like they'd been dipped in blood.

"Just a second, guys." I swallow a handful of amphetamines to get my heart going for practice. The door shakes and there's more shouting. I fall again putting my sweatpants on, then clamber up and grab my baseball gear. "One goddamn second!"

Dizzy and Brian and Justin are in the hallway when I open the door. Justin looks angry. I flutter-wave my fingers like a parade queen but no one laughs. Brian throws a baseball into his mitt. "Ready to go, Hap?" Dizzy asks.

"Yeah, sorry. Taking a nap," I say. All of the warping noise is giving me a headache. It feels like I've been asleep for weeks. I force a grin.

"We gotta go. Now!" Justin shouts, loping down the hall.

"Shit, Chester." Brian yips over his shoulder. "We're gonna be late 'cause of you. Coach will be pissed."

EACH BASEBALL BOOMS; THEY CAROM OFF OF MY CATCHER'S mitt and pummel my forearms and chest protector. My mouth fills with bloody spit after I drop to block a curveball and it shoots up into my face—the mask tears away, burning my chin. Two pitches later, a fastball bounces in front of me and I take it in the ear.

"What kinda lipstick you wearing today?" Tree yells. "Little fuckin' bitch!" He kicks the fake mound. "Shit!" The shout echoes through the Field House. "Who is this fuckin' guy?"

"Fuck you." I say under my breath. "Eat shit. Blow me. Suck a fatty. Die, asshole."

I'm used to being the best. A sweet music usually floods me when I play baseball—my body whirs smoothly, perfectly, when I sprint around the diamond. Gripping the bat. I am wielding lightning. I caress my mitt's leathery pocket and can feel my heartbeat. It is all a part of me. It is all mine.

But right now it feels like I'm filled with asphalt. I can't see.

Tree raises his arms above his head; lifts his left leg into himself, where it hovers for a millisecond; then pushes off of the pitching rubber and thrusts himself toward the plate, whipping the baseball at me with his right arm. I poke the mitt out at his pitches, stabbing at balls, and some ricochet away, blasting off of the concrete wall, but most of them burrow into me.

Justin and Ronnie—two of the other catchers—keep shooting me looks. "What the fuck is wrong with you, Chet? Happy forget how to catch a baseball? Let's go, man."

"Yo, Happy, you OK?"

I try to slap feeling back into my forearms and hands, and then gaze into my mitt. After twisting the laces, I put one of the strings in my mouth, yank it tight, and punch my fist into the leather pocket.

"It's all good," I tell Ronnie, but it feels like my veins are filled with Icy Hot. "Little sweat in my eyes."

"Well, let's go then, playboy," Ronnie laughs. "Happy time." He flips a ball to me but I miss it and it bounces away.

Coach tells me to take a breather so I go to the end of the Field House and sit on a bench. The gym floor is dizzying with colored lines; when we ran wind sprints I thought I was going to tumble headfirst and throw up. I put down as much water as I can and spray the bottle over me. When I lean over the trash can and spit, the ruby phlegm is as thick as yarn. I drop my skullcap over my face and stare into the foam so I don't get the spins. My head is all fucked up. For the rest of practice I listen to my teammates' tinny shouts, the pierce and crack of baseballs and bats and gloves.

"Happy, you coming over tonight?" Rick tips an imaginary bottle to his mouth and then *yeeeeaaaahh*s, refreshed. Everyone in the locker room laughs. "You know you want to," he says. "See you at nine."

"Don't know, man. I got a ton of shit to do before spring break."

"WHAT? This is college, Happy. You got *nothing* better to do," he laughs. "We'll sit around doing econometrics. Nothing better to do."

"Nuthin' at all!" Tom stands in front of the lockers

buck naked, helicoptering a towel over his head. "Nothing at aaaalllllll!" he groans. His voice goes deep, and then he croons. "Eeeeeeconomeeeeeetriiiiiiiiiics!!"

"You're a young buck, Happy," Tree says dully. "You'll learn. Put your Marx in your back pocket, wherever you wake up tomorrow, you'll know it all. Assmosis, my young man."

"Not sure, fellas. Feeling kinda fucked up." I try to laugh, but I have to put my head down and close my eyes. "Got a cold coming on. The flu. Couldn't see nuthin' out there."

"Didn't look like it." Tree laughs sarcastically. "You gotta man up, little bitch!"

"A bad day, Hap," Tom says. "Just don't do it again."

"Shit, you don't need to see anything to have a little fun." Tree saunters through the locker room. "You can feel your way home. All those first-year girls. All those Miss Luckies! Oh, to be young again!" He walks by and shoves me. "Come on, Happy. Come ooooooowwwwn, little bitch!"

Ronnie lifts his fingertips to his lips and inhales. "Who's gonna be the bad guy tonight, Happy? You? You gonna be the bad guy!" He flicks the fantasy joint to the floor and sashays toward the showers. "You *want* to be the bad guy."

"You're always the fucking bad guy, man." I laugh. "I was playing. Course I'm coming over. Someone get me some gin and a case of bottles at Park."

I'm cradling my head when Django slides out of the

shower and fucks the air. He sings high-pitched and dances the cabbage patch, then the running man. He karate-chops the steam. Someone calls him an Ichabod Crane–looking motherfucker.

"HEY, SWEETIE," JULIE SAYS, HOOPING HER ARMS AROUND MY neck and kissing me. My girlfriend stands on the dorm steps, athletic-slim and radiant. Wet, her hair is a deeper shade of blond. I've had a crush on Julie since the first day of college—I saw her smiling in front of the Union and knew she was the one. From that afternoon on, she seemed to be everywhere, appearing like a beautiful tic in the corner of my vision. For months, I inched toward her at parties and caught her eye around campus. I smiled, waiting for the relationship she was in to end, imagining her face on every girl I hooked up with.

"Well, well, well, gorgeous!" I grin.

"How are you, babe?" She takes my hand like I'm escorting her along the balustrade at a ball. "How was practice? Are you getting excited for the first game?"

Lights from the rooms in Turck flutter across the grass. The door clicks locked as we kiss again and her mouth is sugary and warm.

The spring air is steamed milk and metal, and Julie's hand is delicate. I have to focus on the concrete to stay upright.

The lights along the walkway look like fires in the dark, and I'm having trouble making out her words so

HAPPY

I pull her down to a bench. The world is spinning as she scoots under my arm. I close my eyes and run my finger in tiny circles on the back of her head.

"Why are you being so funny?" She leans in and covers my face in kisses. "Hey, you! Silly boy!"

"I'm fine. Just spacin' out. How's your day?" I nest my head on her thighs and stare, unhearing, as she answers. I feel like shit. A pretty mouth is all I see when she talks: a pretty mouth moving, and the stars. I suck on her fingers until she slaps me softly.

When she pauses, I cut in.

"I can't hang out tonight, Jules. I have a ton of work to do. Essays to read and a biodiversity paper to start. I have to go."

"What?" She frowns. "Will you come over when you're done? Lisa is going to be gone."

"I'll try to swing by. OK? I'll call. And think about this weekend." I smile and kiss her again. "We can use Casey's car. Big Head Todd tickets, something at First Avenue. Anything you want. Anything."

SLOUCHED AT MY DESK, I COPY A RILKE POEM—*face to face with the sky*—and e-mail it to Julie, and apologize for being so busy. I promise to make it up to her. The computer wobbles like I'm cross-eyed. The room spins. I send another message to Ma, asking if the ground's thawed enough for planting, if she's working on her sculptures. I tell her that the first baseball games are next week in the Metrodome and I'm excited and nervous, but all of the melting snow seems strange without her around.

Wherever we lived, there'd be a spring Saturday that would find Ma and me standing at the dead garden's edge like Lewis and Clark. She'd press a shovel or a pitchfork into my arms, then lead me around the yard, marking the tree stumps that needed to be dug up, the swath of soil I needed to turn and break apart. Working beside me, she'd sing in the warming air. Hours later, I'd say I was finished and she'd point out what I'd half-assedly missed, the flowers I'd stepped on or dragged the hose over. I'd swear under my breath and go back to halving worms until she gave me permission to leave.

When I shut the computer down, darkness creams across the dorm like I'm in a Dalí painting. I close my eyes and the rustling trees sound like woodwinds.

Brad and Justin smack the walls walking down the hallway toward my room, their laughs subterranean. "Hey, guys," I say loudly when the door starts to open. It stops, and a slant of brightness cuts over the tiles.

"What are you doing in there, Chet? Whacking it?" Justin laughs.

Brad peeks in. "What the hell? ARE YOUR PANTS OFF, AL?" He laughs. "IS THAT YOUR DICK IN YOUR HAND? OH, JEEEEESUS! MY EYES!"

"Don't worry." I turn on the desk lamp and blink up at them. "I just finished, you assholes."

My best friend, Casey, slams through the door a half hour later, flinging condoms like Frisbees. "Gifts for everyone," he sings. "Gifts! Gifts! Gifts!"

16

Happy

"Come in. Mr. Golden. Stewy Gold!" I yell. "Yes, presents! We win! We win!"

Slumped in bed. I drink a beer. Girls scream past our propped-open door. Casey dribbles a basketball back and forth between his legs and Brad and Justin watch TV. Justin talks conservative politics and Indiana, and Casey squawks "Bullshit" each time he tries to make a point. "Wrong, again." Casey laughs. "cock breath."

I feel sick and standing up is a Herculean task, but I smile at my friends. "This, right here." I say, head tilted to the ceiling while I unravel a purple rubber. "is a very good thing."

Brad mutes the television. Casey and Justin stop pushing each other. I exhale dramatically and the room quiets. "All of your hopes and dreams!"

"You fucking chucklehead." Casey wings another condom off of my face and I fall backward into bed and everyone howls. "Fa dushiarchy fun face." he shouts. and spins the basketball on an upright finger.

"Shit. Case." I throw a condom at the ball but miss. "That doesn't even make sense. You're getting all fucking *Finnegans Wake* on us."

They each say "No, thanks" when I ask them if they want to hang out with the upperclassmen, so I pack my backpack with booze and leave.

"Awww shit." I careen into the doorway of Rick's room when I walk in. raining papers and pens from the empty Busch Light boxes they've stacked into an end table. Beer bottles chime in my backpack.

"Easy, Happy." Tom looks up, dead serious. "Get ahold of yourself, man!" he laughs, then shakes my hand.

Tree stares at me, leans to Rick, and says something about the freshman being fucking worthless, just loud enough so everyone can hear it. "Kidding, bradda!" he shouts, punching my arm.

"Man, check your shit." KJ pushes me. "You're fucking bush league! BUSH LEAGUE, HAPPY!"

Rick spits in a bottle, pulls down his hat, and nods hello. "Nice to see you, Happy." He smiles. "Glad ol' Chester got all his shit done."

"Whoo ha!" I yell like Busta Rhymes, punching my fists and forcing myself to laugh. "Whoo haaaaa! I'm canned already. What a fuckin' night! Sorry, fellas." Everyone chuckles watching me fall sideways onto the couch. My head throbs. The world bounces in time with my heartbeat. I hiss a beer open with my key chain, and Rick tosses me a tin of Skoal. When we clink our bottles together it feels like I've got a tuning fork inside my chest.

The drinks spill as we spout our apocrypha, and I tell them how good my life was—the big game, the Super 8, at the farmhouse, the playoffs, in the cornfields, the state tournament, the superhero, the pond, jumping naked off the cliffs. And then the tapioca-thick sex stories—the backseat of a Buick, the church parking lot, a friend's mom's minivan, with the parents upstairs. while my friends pounded the car's steamy windows. under the stars on home plate.

"Moving to Iowa Falls was like going back in time," I say, belching out weed smoke. The light is frayed, grayscale. Empty bottles turret the tabletops.

"BACK IN TIME!" KJ slurs. "Fucking Huey Lewis and the News!

"Fireworks over Riverbend Rally and jumping from motorboats and weed in the ditches. Camping and skinny-dipping when the fire started going out." I go on and on. laughing to myself, eyes sewn shut. "It was like *Grease* or something. Cruising Main Street and fistfights. Dances after football games and homecoming parades. It was all Mayberry and shit."

"MAYBERRY! MOTHERFUCKING MAYBERRY!" KJ yells, standing. He mutters something about pissing and uses the wall to feel his way out of the room.

"It's called Iowa. Happy." Ronnie says. "No bad guys come from Iowa Falls. Not until Happy Lemon! Yeah. playa!" He laughs and nods, then says that nothing was better than SoCal back in the day.

"Stockton." Tree says solemnly. and pretends to pour his beer on the floor. "Get that shit right."

"Shiiiiiit. bro!" Ronnie leans back into the couch and smiles. "Fuck that place."

I laugh and keep talking, but hardly anyone is listening anymore. Tom and Tree and Ian are watching TV and playing cards. KJ comes back and passes out cold. and Ronnie is blazed. I chug and mumble to myself about fields of soybeans and corncribs in the moonlight. Gravel jamming through the countryside in old Chevelles. Getting high and the Doors and tripping our balls off and Black Sabbath.

"We had fucking birds in the freezer, man."

"What the fuck did you say, Happy?" Ian turns.

"Pull it together, man! You're hardly speaking English."

Everyone is looking at me.

"Birds. We had dead ones . . . dead birds in the freezer. I'd get some ice, and there one would be. Dead grackles, man. A house finch. Fucking birds, you know? A bird. Wings and beaks and shit? Birds."

"GRACKLE!" KJ is awake again. "Fucking grackles. That's crazy good."

"You serious? That's fucked up is what it is."

"Loco shit, Happy." Ronnie laughs. "But my moms had a taco stand!"

"What? A taco van?"

"GRACKLE!"

"Naaaw, I'm playing, you fool! Fucking taco stand." Ronnie slaps his thigh. "Jesus, no, silly fucks. It was all concrete jungle for me. Ghetto birds!"

"CAAAWWW! CAAAAWWWW!"

"We had birds in the freezer."

"Happy's studying too much, it's making him hallucinate. He thinks he's fucking Audubon."

"Assholes." I pick a shred of loose chew from my lip. "Ma and Bob are artists, man. We had wild shit—bowling balls rolling around the floors, busted mirrors on the walls. Snakeskins tacked above the dinner table. It was awesome." I shake my head and try to laugh it off. I don't usually talk to my teammates about how I was raised because I want to fit in with them. "Fuckin' loved it." I smile, but part of me has always resented it.

"Happy, you're a goofy bastard. You know that, homes?"

In the morning, bottles and ash are fanned across my desk. The drawer is wrenched open: Rx bottles, painkillers, pep pills, pens, and a baggie of weed. I teeter down the hallway and find Casey shaving in the bathroom. Behind him, I pirouette around the wet floor.

"Well, if it ain't the one and only Willy Lump Lump." He runs a razor down his chin. "And how are you on this shittastic morning?"

"Don't fuck up, Case." I yell. I jump around, mess up my hair. "Don't cut up that Jay Leno chin of yours." I laugh in his ear. "Don't fuck it up, man."

He drops the razor into the foamy sink and stares at me in the mirror. "What the fuck do you *want*, Lemon?"

"Nothing." I wolf-whistle, trying to remember what happened last night.

"You sure?"

I nod.

"All right then. Leave me the fuck alone. I'm working here, pal."

2

"Ali Baba, this is your Ma. Call your Ma, Ali," she warbles on the message. "Call me call me call me call me. Ma Ma Ma Ma Ma. Call call call. Me me me me." She's still rambling, saying she loves me and banging pots and pans, when the machine cuts her off.

Brad's gone and our room is a cesspool. I can't remember if I saw him this morning.

For a week I've felt like an aquarium filled with mercury and belly-up goldfish. I can't shake it off. Each baseball practice is a brand-new beat-down.

I rest against the cool cement wall and listen to the message again. "Ali Baba, this is your Ma. Call your Ma, Ali." A withered plant is toppled next to a box fan on the windowsill. Mold like piecrust. "Ma Ma Ma Ma Ma. Call call call. Me me me me."

Students are lounging outside, sitting in the grass and standing in groups on the walking path. It's finally getting beautiful in Minnesota. Trees are sucking winter up through their roots, exploding luscious and green.

All last summer Ma had packed for her next move. She'd only take breaks to come watch my ballgames, trying to see as many as she could before blowing out of Iowa Falls. I was so excited to leave for college—to finally be out of the house—that I hardly helped her. I was pumped—since she was moving before the season finished, I got to live with Jonny for a month.

I came home after the last game Ma came to and she was standing in the room where all of her records had been. Her chin was tucked to her chest like the guitar in her arms was whispering. A crown that came out of the bronze mold with QUELN on it instead of QUEEN squatted on the homemade bookshelf behind her. A box filled with all of the drawings and paintings and sculptures I'd made for her was splayed open on the floor.

She plucked a string, listened, and then twisted a tuning key. The late afternoon sky reflected off of the guitar's body, and her face, usually red from hours of gardening, was the color of honey. Her long white hair was latticed with light. She slid her fingers down the frets, strummed big one time like a rock star, and started singing the Bonnie Raitt song she always listened to in her art studio.

We had lived in that tumbledown duplex on Bliss Boulevard for four years—the longest we lived anywhere—and Ma is a hoarder. Acrylics and charcoal and pastels and crayons, piles of scraps she was saving for sculptures and collage. There was a shitload of books—science and health safety texts from the '50s, the history of everything, art of the world, atlases of countries that no longer exist, and a partial set of Funk and Wagnalls encyclopedias. There was ancient hi-fi equipment, an orchestra's worth of instruments. A dozen cracked bowling balls. Spider plants. Wandering Jew. Gardening trays of zinnias and begonias and black-eyed Susans. Cut-in-half plastic bottles—green leaves sprouting through the dirt. Christmas cactus. Snakeskins. Horseshoe crab shells, beetle husks, and duck wings. Two printing presses and wall-sized sheets of slate. Hundred-pound boxes of letterpress type and thirteen-foot-long shovels. The house teemed.

THE PHONE RINGS FOR A MINUTE BEFORE MA ANSWERS.

"Hey, Ma! Yo yo Ma! It's me. What's happening?"

"Oh, Al, I'm so happy it's you! I thought you might be the fucking guy who always calls when I'm eating, trying to sell me shit. I was ready to hang up. How ya doing, laddie?"

"I'm doing good, doing good. Same old stuff. What about you, Ma? How's Missouri?"

"Ooooooh, fine," she says in an Irish brogue. "Working on some new collages. My students are making cardboard chairs this week." She talks excitedly about her new job.

"Good, Ma. Awesome."

"But are you sure you're OK?" Her voice slows. "You sound like something's up. What's happening?"

"Nothing, Ma. Things are fine."

She keeps talking, asking if I'm OK, and I look outside. The sun glows through the girls' sundresses and I can see all the way up their blacked-out legs. Every branch on the trees looks like it's about to break, heavy and surging with robins and black squirrels.

"Just tired." I say when she finally quiets. "Got the flu or something. Sore throat. I'm working too hard and not sleeping enough. Eyes are weird. I'm playing ball like crap."

"Doesn't sound like the flu. You need to get your rest, and—"

"I know, Ma! I know. I know. Fuuuuuck. You don't get it. Mac's a little different than high school." I try to laugh because it came out mean, but I can't stand when she lectures me. "I have to reread stuff, you know? Spend time researching, proofreading and shit. Ugh. You know, Ma? It's hard work!"

She makes an exasperated noise. "You spent too much time playing football and lifting weights. I don't care if you were good. Oh, I hated that shit. Stupid, stupid shit. You shoulda been doing more homework and shoveling snow. Digging up stumps in the yard! That's what you shoulda been doing. That's a fact, jack!"

"Maaaaaa!" I groan.

"Did you ever show me homework? Shit," she says, "did you even have any?"

"Nope. Never. That's why you didn't see it, Ma. So sad, too bad."

I laugh and she says, "Bullshit," but I know she's smiling. "You need me to be up there to ground your ass. Then you'd get some shit done. You taking your vitamins?"

"Ma. I'm taking them."

"Are you sure? I'll send more."

"I'm taking 'em!" I grab two vitamin bottles and shake them into the phone like maracas. "See, see, see!" I drown her out, and she quiets.

"Hey, Ma, when you talk to Bob tell him that I love him, OK? Gotta go. Love ya."

"OK, love you too, Ali. Be good."

Just before I hang up I hear her voice like it's coming from beneath my bed: "Ali, Ali, Ali, Ali! Wait, wait, wait! Forgot something! Gotta tell you something!"

"Yeah, Ma? What is it?" I sigh, pressing the phone back to my ear. "Yeah?"

"Hey, Ali!"

"Yeah, Ma? What?"

"Ali! Love you, Ali. Love you. Call any time you want, OK? Now go to bed!" She laughs. "You're grounded, so go to bed! Now!"

It's three in the afternoon.

THE NEXT MORNING, I TUMBLE HEADLONG IN THE SHOWER and, trying to catch myself, bend a fingernail back.

Happy

Water pounds down. Cold tiles when I kneel, crumple. Bloody spit dangles from my chin. Around me, the stall whiplashes. I slump against the wall, half close my eyes, and tilt my head back so the stream pelts my face.

3

"I TELL YOU, MAN. I WAS FUCKING ACCOSTED," IAN SAYS, BIT-
ing into a veggie burger at lunch. "Right there by my
car. Thought they were going to shoot me. Fucking
hoodlums in this city. Hoodlums."

"You're full of shit, Shaw." My teammates throw
food and make faces. " 'Accosted'? What the fuck is
that, man? What does that even mean? They shove
something up your ass? Bet you liked it."

It's been four days since I fell in the shower, and the
blackened fingernail is barely hanging on. I chew at it
while Ian talks. The dried blood tastes like salt and
mustard. The hoots get louder. I can't feel the fork in
my hand. I close my eyes and everything spins, slowly
at first, and then the table feels like it's rushing up at
my face.

"I swear, man. That kind of shit doesn't happen
where I'm from. Not back in Corvallis, homes," Ian

says seriously. He tries to look devastated and the laughs get louder. "You shouldn't have to worry about that shit. I was accosted, man. I can't believe it!"

The bloody moon rests in a dome of saliva after I spit it out on the table.

"*Can you believe that, homes?*" Tree sneers, mimicking Ian. "Shit." He hop-steps like he's going to dance but just picks up his lunch tray and looks down at our table with big, surprised eyes. "*Accosted,* homes!" he shouts. "IF I'M LYING, I'M DYING!"

At dinner, Casey groans at my fingernail. "Hide that shit, man. It's been winking at me this whole time." He ring-tosses his Phillies hat over it, pushes his plate away from him. "Al, I can't eat."

"What? This?" I boomerang his hat to the floor and wriggle the finger in his face. "This thing?"

He slaps my hand away, picks his hat up, and angles it atop his head. His fingers pinch down the bill like he's squeezing juice out of it. "What happened to that shit? Julie got snapping pussy?"

"You asshole. Happened at practice, took a pitch off the finger."

"Yeah, well, if you didn't suck so bad you might be OK. Now look, you've gone and got yourself Ebola finger. All you gotta do is catch the fucking ball, Lemon. Easy as pie."

Casey and I were laughing hysterically within minutes of meeting each other this fall. After orientation-day icebreakers, we wisecracked about the other first-year assholes living with us in Dayton Hall. The dick-nosed boy and the guy with butt-length hair who'd been stuffed into the lounge because there wasn't a room for him. The tweaky RA who smiled coolly and openly stared at the girls' tits. Casey dribbled a basketball as we walked around campus, talking about snowboarding and Pennsylvania girls. Once it was clear that we were going to be good friends, we stopped posturing and he chuckled and told me he'd been a chubby kid. Each time he did a sit-up during the Presidential Fitness Test in elementary school, his fat self straining up and down as fast as he could go, he'd fart—*poot, poot, poot*—and the boy holding his feet would scream.

As the August dusk had closed around us, I told Casey that Ma had raised me by herself and we'd lived all over the states. "Got some free lunch for a while," I laughed. "Government cheese, bitches!" I talked about growing up in art departments, inventing games with dice and baseball cards and stats, and Chairball—a couple of rolling chairs, a cardboard hoop, and a beach ball—while Ma welded or hammered white-hot steel. I told him that her face looked like a sunburned shovel the night my high school principal stopped by to let us know that I was suspended. I had punched his son, Rocky—one of my good friends—in the face, then yelled and watched him bleed. While Rocky went to the doctor because of his cut eye, I had ridden my bike around Iowa Falls trying to figure out what to tell Ma. She wouldn't stop hugging me when I finally walked in the art building at the college; she was so overjoyed that I couldn't tell her I had attacked my friend. I walked my bike to our house, guilt parching my insides. The phone rang all afternoon and I ignored it. When Ma got home, I served dinner and she turned the ringer off because answering the phone during meals was forbidden. But I knew I was fucked when I saw Mr. Robbins's car pull into the driveway. Ma came back to the table after answering the door and asked, "So that's why you weren't at football practice? That's why you came to see me?" She sighed. "You're grounded for two months."

Casey and I sat on the bench in front of Dayton that first day of college, and he said I should have ducked out the back that night and lived off the fat of the land. "I can already tell you'd have been a great hobo." He grinned. "Fucking Knapsack Jones."

But sitting in a booth that night at dinner, I can't tell him how sick I've been feeling.

"Fuck you, Golden." I smile. "I've seen you swing a bat, chump. You suck balls."

"All I do is hit home runs."

"Bullshit." I wrap the sandwich I've made for later in a napkin. "But man, I've been playing like shit. Can't do nothing right."

"That excited for spring break, huh?"

"I'm fucking bad right now. Never played like this."

"Like Michael Jackson?"

"Man, you're a fucking idiot." I laugh. "Bad, like your girlfriend's rash."

After I ask him to get me some oranges, he stands and grabs his nuts. Laughing evilly, he *Thriller*s off to the dessert bar. My headache comes back with a vengeance; the plates, the silverware, mouths slurping down drinks, all of the chewing and talking—everything in the dining hall is excruciatingly loud.

I catch Julie's eye when she walks in with her soccer teammates and mouth that I'll stop by later. Casey drops an orange on the table and I smile sheepishly.

"You're whipped already, Al," he says, sliding into the booth. "Don't fuck it up, Lemon! It's too soon to go down in flames!"

"Goldfarb, you don't know shit."

"It's true." He rolls oranges across the table and they plop in my lap. "Pussy whipped."

"No way. You're jealous."

"Oh no!" he laughs. "She's not my type, and *you*, my good friend, are pussy whipped." Casey spoons up his ice cream while I stuff the fruit and tuna sandwich in my pockets. "I'm a toilet seat, Al. You should be out there getting ass! LIKE ME! LIKE A CHAMPION!"

"I'll knock the champion out." I smile, slowly kiss each of my fists. He shakes his head no and snatches my last orange. "So, Case, can I borrow your car this weekend or what? That be cool?"

"Oh, so you've moved beyond the whipping of the pussy stage and now it's love? Whip that shit!" He laughs and whips his arm above him. "Yeah, sure, take it, man. No problemo."

"Thanks, Case."

"Don't sweat it." His spoon scrapes the bowl. "What's up with you anyway, man? Why you been such a jackass lately? All *I Spy* and shit."

"Nothing."

"Bullshit." He shakes his head. After scooping ice cream, he looks around the dining hall and then stares at me, waiting.

"Just feeling out of it, I guess. I got the flu or something. A sore throat. You know? Fucking been getting them all year. I'm run down, man."

"Come on, really?"

When Casey's sick I hop around his bed screaming songs from *The Wizard of Oz*. Wrestling his shoulders, I ask if his feline AIDS has flared up. I slap his legs and call him a pussy-assed bitch, tear the blankets away, and tell him to get his sorry ass up. I sing circus music and polka-clap.

"I'm fuckin' fine, man."

On the way out we smile and wave at the lunch lady who always asks "What are you having?" before she dishes up our food.

"You boys!" She grins to the man next to her, says, "Those funny boys!"

"She sounds like fuckin' Bobcat Goldthwait." I laugh and drop my tray on the conveyor belt.

Casey takes a final sip of his drink. "Gremlin-assed bitch."

Hopping down the steps, he says, "I don't believe you." He looks back up at me because I'm moving so slowly, says, "Your finger. You were fucking wasted, weren't you? Good ol' Blackout Jenkins. Probably fell down and fucked your shit up like you do each week-end."

"Ha, ha, ha." I kick open the door and try to tackle him. "*What are you having,* motherfucker?"

4

THE BASEBALL IS AN ARCING PUCKER OF CRIMSON AND TAN AS it curves toward where I'm crouched. And then my vision jumps. The ball I'm supposed to catch vanishes, and I can't see shit. So I do exactly what Coach says: I slide my chest in front of where I think the pitch is going and the ball recoils off the ground and hits me in the throat. Four pitches later Kurt throws a slider in the dirt and it bounces up and rocks my face mask and whizzes away.

"Way to get in front of it, Chet," Coach yells. "But you gotta block that ball. You can't let it get away from you." His voice hardens. "That's how we lose games. Come on now, Chet! Keep that sucker in front of you. Each one that gets away is a loss!"

Nodding at Coach, I lower into my catcher's stance, trying to make out Kurt's shape on the mound. It looks like he's got eight arms. Four gloves, four baseballs, all of them flickering. Flashing him signs, I start to tip, and instead of hiding my throwing hand behind my back, I plant it beside me like a kickstand. Kurt's arm lassos toward me. I'm supposed to be good at this. I've always been an all-star. But there's no way Coach is going to put me in the lineup in the first games.

The last two weeks the ground to my right has been rushing toward my face. The Field House blurs around me, and I go hours without being able to feel my body, confused, trying to figure out what's happening around me. Inside me.

When I step into the cage, I slice the bat through the air and then wait, the Easton resting on my right shoulder. My neck muscles tense when Coach releases the first ball. His elbow stretches rubbery and his fingers press a white smear from his opening hand. The comet screams toward me, and I start my hips, but when the ball is halfway to the plate, my vision jumps again. The baseball disappears. My eyes roll in their sockets, and everything between Coach and me goes blurry. It's like he hasn't yet thrown the pitch. Like there is no ball at all. I feel myself falling, legs quivering to right myself, and then, suddenly, the baseball appears right in front of me, shooting celestially through the watercolored light, snipping over the dish. The ball hits the net, and I've barely started to swing. The guys watching hoot and clap and I shout, "Fucking shit!" and toss the bat off of the ground.

"Happy, you're swinging like a bitch." KJ laughs. "Let's go, man. Punish that shit!" He sticks a bat between his legs and thrusts his hips. "PUNISH IT, MAN!" He makes gorilla noises. "Get primitive on that shit!"

"Blind man could hit better than you, Hap," Flynn says when I whiff at the next one. "Did you forget what that thing in your hands is? It's called a bat. We're playing a game called baseball. You're up there swinging your dick, man. Jesus."

"Not so good," Kawika grumbles. "Dang. Looking not so good, brah."

I'm sneaking out of the locker room when Dizzy stops me. "Hey, Hap," he says, cleaning his glasses with a towel, "we're playing cards tonight if you want to come by."

"Yeah, Diz, thanks. I might." I smile. "Going home so I can sit in my own shower with some cold beers. Better than this sausage party." I laugh meekly and wave. "See you fucks at dinner."

Under the shower's cold water, blood riots through my skin. Bruises map my body.

JULIE'S ROOM IS STROBE-LIT IN THE MORNING. THE BED-spread is too bright, ruffled and yellow around us. She kisses my nose and bites my ear. "You should get your-self looked at," she says, straddling me. She makes a stern face. "Call today."

Last night in the candle-fluttering dark, she said, "You'll love this," turned a CD on, and then slipped back under the sheets. Listening to Calobo, we kissed and finger-drummed each other's chests and after the CD finished, she told me about going to one of their concerts at the Crystal Ballroom. I promised to bring over a CD she hadn't heard and then asked about her home. She talked about her parents and uncle and Oma and Opa and Holland soccer and Portland's Rose Gardens. I told her about the albums I'd just bought and how shopping at Cheapo Records reminded me of going to the library with Ma when I was little. How I listened to *Old Yeller* until the record player needle was dull, but my favorites, the ones I sang over and over as a boy, were the Irish drinking songs—the Clancy Brothers and Tommy Makem. *"Whiskey, you're the devil, you're leading me astray, over the hills and mountains and to Amerikay,"* I sang, stumble-dancing around in my underwear as Julie laughed. We described our favorite Dale Chihuly sculptures by tracing our tongues over each other's stomachs. Later, she asked if I'd visit her this summer and I said yes. The dark quieted and after a while, I told her that I haven't been feeling well. She held my hand, asking questions until I said I didn't want to talk about it anymore. Julie slept all night, mouth plum and half-open, while I tossed and turned.

She slides off of me and stands next to the bed, naked in the morning light. "Don't you think you should? Al? Are you even listening to me?"

"I think I'll wait it out. I need to sweat more. Toxins, be gone!"

"I think you should go to the health clinic. I'm sure

they'll see you right away and you'll be fine. It'll only take a second."

She pulls a pair of panties and a bra from the drawer, drops them on her desk, and then puts on a robe. "You should do it right now. Call them."

"I'm gonna go soon." My mouth feels needled with Novocain. "Probably should do it before spring break, right? Hey, can I borrow that CD?"

She holds her shower caddy like a purse, steps into the hallway. "Please do it. And yes. Of course."

"Thank you, gorgeous."

When she gets back, she turns the stereo on and starts humming. Showerheat clots the room. Aveda and lavender body wash. I prop myself up and watch the robe drop to the floor.

"What are you looking at?" she asks coyly, toweling her head.

"Just thinking about political science." I try to look innocent.

Teasingly slow, she bends over and dries her legs.

"Hey, Jules."

"What?" Her stomach is flat and soft and flawless; I want to hibernate inside her.

"You don't need to go to class, do you?" I fling my arms open wide. She feigns annoyance when I sing in a bad show-tune voice. "Not this morning, right?"

"Hmmm." She tries to look concerned.

"Come back! Now, for shit's sake, now!"

"I don't know." She smiles, walking back to bed.

5

Nurse Bob is a biker-looking dude—ZZ Top beard, a bunch of earrings, and a ponytail—in a lab coat. He asks me what's been going on with a grin and then leans forward like he wants me to know he cares.

"Oh, you know, last two weeks or so, I've been a little dizzy. Eyes are funny." I look at the cuts on my hands. "I just feel strange."

He nods and writes. "Tell me more."

"Like things are moving around and stuff, and I'm going to fall down. Not right, or something, I don't know. Things are really loud. Bright. My face feels funny." I smile as wide as I can. "I'm probably, like, fine, you know? It's just weird."

He shines a light in my eyes and has me track his finger to the left and right. He looks in my mouth and ears, then steps back and rests his fists on his hips like a superhero.

Happy

People are shuttling around the waiting room next door. A morning bus brakes outside on Grand Avenue. His words snuffle. I can't focus.

Nurse Bob scribbles in my file, then hands me a prescription and a note. "Get these, start taking them today." He smiles big. "Come back to the health clinic if you're not feeling better in a week."

After weaving back to campus from the pharmacy, I lay in the grass in front of Old Main, staring into the vibrating trees, pretending to sleep when anyone walks by. I roll to my belly and watch the pills crawl across my palm. "For my inner-ear infection," I say. "My flu." I settle them on my tongue and swallow stale water from my Nalgene until they spread in my throat like a sandstorm.

Walking into the hallway after my political science class that afternoon, I plow into the plastic recycling bins. I lean against the wall while my classmates laugh. Gripping the railing like it's a lifeline, I inch myself down the two flights of stairs to get outside.

GETTING OUT OF BED IN THE MORNING, I FALL DOWN AGAIN, hard. I bumble to the phone. "When is the medicine supposed to kick in?" I ask the woman who answers at the health clinic. It's been over two weeks since I first crashed to the floor.

"What do you mean?"

"How long before the medicine makes me feel better? The pills I got yesterday."

"What's your name again? I need to look at your file."

Outside, campus is blindingly green. Students are laughing and rushing to class, a mayhem of sound and light, stretched out like taffy and receding from me. I have to look away from the windows. Papers rustle on the other end. I lie on the floor and fold the dirty rug under my chin.

"You should start feeling better right away."

The rug smells like piss. Next door, the RA is blaring house music. Beneath my bed, a dirty cup quivers on the tiles.

"I want to see someone else."

The line quiets.

"You could visit with the doctor, if you'd like. He comes to campus for appointments today."

"The what?"

"The doctor."

A MINUTE INTO THE APPOINTMENT, THE DOCTOR FLATTENS MY tongue until I gag and taste soiled couch. I cough as he smiles and throws the wooden stick into the trash like he's shooting hoops. When I'm done hacking, he tugs my earlobe, shoves a black cone in one ear, and then gazes into my skull. He *hmmm*s, says it looks a little pink, maybe infected, and then puts his hand on my upper back. The stethoscope is a cool ring when I deep-breathe against his palm. He plucks the lymph nodes on my neck and armpit. When he looks into my eyes, his face screws short. "Your eyes are bouncing," he says, watching them tick.

"Yep. I know." I smile and swallow down my anger. "Been doing that for a couple of weeks. Everything's moving."

While I scratch a scab on my hand, he nods. "Probably just an infection," he says kindly. "It is a little pink in your ear canal, a little pink. Probably nothing to worry about." He smiles. "Probably. Any time there's an infection and the vestibular system is affected, it can make you feel very off. Day-to-day things can become extremely difficult. Almost impossible."

Canals and redness and swelling, he goes on, and I stop listening. I have to get out of here.

". . . but because it has the potential to be something serious, very serious, you need to see someone else."

"Why?" I ask, disgusted.

"Because all of this could be neurological," he says—and now each word sounds like a brick crashing through the clinic window. "You need to see a specialist to be sure." A pen clicks. He flips through papers. "We need to get you a neurologist appointment right away. We'll arrange one for this afternoon." He smiles. "Just to be safe."

Afterward, I sit on a bench in the sun with my eyes half-closed, headphones on. Students wheel around the walkways. Jumbles of oak shadows and muffled sounds. Under the cottony light it feels like I'm on a ship, pitching from side to side.

I only played a half inning of our first games. Cowering at the end of the dugout, I hoped Coach wouldn't say anything to me because of the balls I couldn't catch in warm-ups. Every other inning, I felt my way down the stadium hallway and sat in the dark bathroom.

"Doctor said it was an inner-ear infection," I tell my teammates, stripping down in the locker room. My eyes are closed so I don't get sick. "No big deal." The room fills with the usual laughs. Cussing guffaws and spitting and shit-talking.

"Yeah? That's great, Happy." I have no idea who's talking to me.

"The medicine is kicking in," I laugh, and slide an orange sweatband up my forearm. "'Bout fucking time, huh?"

"Thank God, Hap. You couldn't play much worse, right? Fuck, man. Fucking shitty."

"You going to finally be a playa, huh, playboy?" Ronnie shouts. "Happy the bad guy! The motherfucking smooth criminal!"

In three days, spring break starts, and we're going to Florida for a week of games. I know the sunshine will make me better. My body will be a perfect machine, and I'll smash pitches into the power alleys for doubles. I'll steal bases and block each bouncing changeup.

"Spring break, fuckers!" I slam my locker door and grin. "And the party, O! Strippers, my strippers! Shit . . . I'm feeling better already."

HAPPY

I try to look deep in thought, but I have to steady myself on the bench when I grab my mitt. A garbage can rainbows from the other side of the lockers. Paper towels flutter down and the trash bin bongs off of the floor. David shrugs, picks it up, and tosses it back.

"Shit, brudda!" Tree points his index fingers out from his nipples and then starts to swing them around. He starts to thrust his pelvis and moan and everyone hoots and catcalls. Tree's fingers rotate: "*Ooooooooh daddy!*" he yells, dancing out the door.

It's peaceful and beige around me for a minute, and then I'm sweating profusely, glued to the examination table's butcher paper. The room is stifling, and when the neurologist turns the lights down, it's a charred jar dropped over me. He leans at me and I flinch and laugh uncomfortably. I tongue the canker sores in my mouth. When I open my eyes he's an inch from my face, exhaling against my chapped lips. Shining a pen-light in my face, he swings his finger in front of my eyes.

Breathing loud and measured like he's deep in a dreamless sleep, Dr. Floberg watches my eyes dart and bob. He asks me to stop blinking, but the harder I try to track his finger the more my eyes jump. Again—"Try not to blink, Alex."

"I am."

"Talk to me about what brings you here," he says, walking quickly to the wall. "Tell me how you've been

45

feeling." It feels like I'm falling from a merry-go-round when the room brightens.

"I'm doing pretty well, I guess."

"Why are you visiting me then?" he asks seriously.

I mumble my litany of symptoms. Dr. Floberg glances up from the file he's writing on but looks out the window behind me.

"We're probably going to have to do a spinal tap," he says nonchalantly. The file hangs loosely from his armpit. "Unless, of course, an MRI shows us something tangible. You'll need to get one right away."

I stare at him; I don't know what the fuck he's talking about, the spinal tap or the MRI. Lowering my eyes, I kick my legs out spastically. "But what do you mean?" My throat is so dry. "What's a spinal tap?"

He explains the procedure, and I imagine—can feel—the enormous needle pushing through the paper-thin skin over my spine. He talks and jabs the air with his finger. "We need to start ruling things out to figure out what's going on with you. It could be multiple sclerosis," Dr. Floberg says. "That's one of the first things we need to look into. Your symptoms could be the result of any number of very serious medical conditions. We need to find out what's causing these issues you're having. It could be a tumor, or a lesion on your spinal cord or brain. A brain hemorrhage or a vascular malformation. Cancer, blood clot, stroke, or bleed."

I can't tell if I'm shaking or nodding with understanding.

"There are a number of things we need to look into. And we need to figure this out right away. You've waited far too long to get looked at. But you are here now, that's the most important thing."

"Yeah . . . OK. So . . . so, what do I do?" I'm a bob-blehead doll of myself.

"We'll figure it out." He smiles. "First things first, we'll get you an MRI."

Dr. Floberg speaks over his shoulder as he writes, then holds a phone to his ear. His jaw moves but I can't hear anymore.

Being in his office is surreal: I haven't been sick since I had chicken pox in sixth grade. I was uninsured until two months ago, when Ma found out that my father hadn't purchased health care for me. She called him all day, every day, until he got it for me.

Dr. Floberg sets the black receiver down and turns. "And you can't go anywhere until we know what's wrong. We need to get some tests done, and then, hopefully, we'll have some good answers for you."

"What?"

"You can't go to Florida on Saturday unless we know what's going on. You need to get an MRI as soon as you can. Tonight, probably. Joan is working on it right now. The only open time might be past midnight, but you need to get it done. It could be nothing, but Alex, your symptoms are very serious. You shouldn't go anywhere. Not until we find out. OK?"

"Are you sure? I think I'm fine."

"This is serious," he says tersely, eyes hard and

unblinking. "Maybe we'll know in two days, but for now, no baseball. Don't do anything."

The elevator doors glide apart, and then I'm standing on Smith Avenue, jumping up and down on the sidewalk so blood will wash back into my legs. Stomach butterflies smokestack up my head. I check my watch, then dig through my backpack for my CD player and headphones and flask. Opening my mouth, I let the wind fill my cheeks. A pipe and a film canister of weed are rolled in a short sock at the bottom of the bag. Practice will be over by the time I get back to campus, so I duck around the corner, pack the bowl, and smoke up—pretending to look for something in the alley's cardboard boxes.

"Here, kitty kitty," I singsong between the tokes. "Here, Biggie. Here, Biggie."

I skip from the alley and beam at the suit-clad men who're walking by. I grin and cough and wave. Blue tie. Red tie. Cool air and sunshine as I laugh my way to the bus stop. Smiling and leaping up the steps, I say "Howdy" to the driver and clink my quarters into the meter. The bus is almost full with weary nine-to-fivers, but there's an empty seat in the very back. The seatback keyed apart, old foam torn out. After taking a few nips, I stuff a chew in my lip, pull the baseball hat down, and lean against the window.

THE WET PAVEMENT IS IRIDESCENT THAT NIGHT; GRAND AVE-nue's two A.M. streetlamps drop pyramids of orange light through the mist. I yell, "Spring break!" climbing into Casey's Blazer, but it's a fatigued bleat. The car is quiet except for our breathing, Julie's nails against the window. Casey yawns. Grand Avenue's buildings fly past us, just fractures of brightness in the smeary dark.

"Philadelphia, man," Casey says, finger-tocking the steering wheel. "The Roots and Eagles and cheesesteaks. That's what we need to do, Al. Cheesesteaks. Sell them shits out of an RV. Don't ya think? They got taco stands in Cali. Minnesota needs something, right? We'll be the Donkel Brothers. We'll rock that shit. Get your fucking cheesesteaks, yo!"

I reach behind the seat and touch Julie's ankle until she wrestles my hand away. She plays my neck with her fingers. "That's a bad idea, Al." Julie laughs and squeezes my shoulders in mock horror. "Don't listen to Casey! Ugh! Cheesesteak. Uuuuuugggghhhhhh! They just sound gross."

Casey turns to me, smiles, and says, "The fucking Donkel Brothers," like Al Pacino in Donnie Brasco. "Fuhgedaboudid," he says. The Blazer swerves when he punches me in the shoulder. "Delicious cheesesteaks! Fucking hmmm-hmmm good!"

We drive over the I-35 overpass and a car whizzes by with one headlight out. Downtown St. Paul is half-lit and drizzly; it looks like an enormous diamond has been ground to dust over it. The smell of the Mississippi River and brewing beer. No one speaks.

"Man, I'm fuckin' asleep!" Casey yawns again. He blasts the stereo—"Let Me Clear My Throat"—to keep us up. He pulls his hat down over his eyes like a trucker and scrunches up his face, then leans over the wheel and says, "Hey there, good buddy, ten-four, niner," and "Whooooeee!" as fast as he can.

I shake my head, smile at Julie.

In the parking lot, we sit in the booming noise with our seat belts on. All of us look like we've been sketched in charcoal. Casey grins and his teeth glint. I turn the CD player off, and it's so quiet, everyone must be holding their breath. No one wants to open a door.

Brooonnngggg! Brooonnngggg! Casey lays on the horn. "Let's do this shit!" he yells. "Poppa needs to go back to bed!"

We goof through the empty waiting room before deciding on seats in a row facing away from the TV. I touch Julie's fingertips with my index finger.

"Everything will be fine, Al." She pushes my neck with the side of her head, prodding me to put an arm around her. "Will you wake me up before you go back there?"

Casey walks laps around the waiting room, swinging his arms and singing softly to himself. The Traditions, the a capella group he's in at Mac, has a concert in Chicago over spring break. Each time he passes I catch phrases of "Masturbating Over You," one of their most popular songs.

"You got to cut that shit out," I laugh when he starts singing "Poison" by Bel Biv DeVoe. He sings louder and starts to thunder-clap from side to side. I laugh and tell him to shut the fuck up, but Julie doesn't move. Her closed eyelids flutter like a wren's chest.

Happy

Over and over Casey looks at the door, then peers over his shoulder at the tube. He plays with his baseball hat, spinning it around his head a bunch of times before burying a hand in the pocket of his hoodie. He plays with his earrings, then licks a finger and rubs at a scuff mark on his white old-school Nikes.

"I need to brush these fuckers. Al, you bring your toothbrush?"

Casey stands, holding his hands like he's going to pray, and then huffs and says he's going out to have a smoke.

The woman behind the desk says "Alex Lemon" loudly to the empty room. She doesn't look up, just hands me the clipboarded papers. Sitting in the chair in front of her, I scribble across the forms. Name. DOB. Address. Doctor. Place of Birth. Allergies. Medications. Surgeries. Why You Are Here. Next to the generic drawing of a hollowed-out man, there are directions to circle and shade-in where it hurts. I don't know what to do. The letters swim.

Casey reeks of smoke when I get back, and Julie is awake. She presses my hands between her legs. She whispers in my ear, but I can't hear anything. I smile, tell her she's beautiful, but the waiting room light is making us all look like corpses. When I get up again, the plastic-covered chair crackles like ice.

As soon as the changing-room door closes behind me I sit on the floor, shaking. I've never been sick.

"You OK?" the woman says on the other side of the door. "Hello? Alex? Whenever you're ready," she says impatiently.

I mumble, look at the time. It's been ten minutes.

The hallway's chemical scent made my nostrils burn, and I have a headache again. I pat my leopardy bruises, take my earring out, pull my T-shirt off, toss everything into the cabinet and lock it. I slip into the blue and white gown. The room spins around me after I stand.

When I open the door, she looks me up and down.

"I look like wallpaper." I smile. "Don't I?"

With a hand already out in front of her, she asks for the cabinet key. I hand it over, and for a few seconds, she stares at the bruises, then starts walking away. "OK, then. Follow me."

Our feet move crisply on the tiles and I tell her that I've never done this before—that I've never even been in a hospital. I talk about Florida, how excited I am for spring break, but she doesn't say a word. We enter another spectacularly white room filled with medical equipment, and through a door-window I see the machine, a body-sized tray extending from it like a diving board. The brightness makes the radiologist who's going to monitor the MRI look like he's quivering, like I'm watching him from the other side of a bonfire.

"How are you? Ready to get started?" The MRI hums and gulps. "Why don't you get in there?" His words start to speedball. "Youneedtobestillwhenyou're inthere." He's not moving his mouth. "Areyouclaustrophobic? Anymetalinyourbody?"

"Not that I know of," I wheeze.

"I'llberightthere," he says, pointing to a darkened window. After I lie down in the tray, he straps my head down. "I'mgonnaputyouinnow. You'llbegreat. Justfine. OK?"

I smile up at him, but I'm terrified. My muscles are cramping. The tray slides into the machine and the radiologist's voice grows distant. I close my eyes. I have never been sick. I don't know what this is. The plastic ceiling is inches above my face.

"I'mgoingtoputsomemusiconOK? Niceandeasy. Niceandeasy. YoudoingOK?"

"I'm fine," I snap bitchily. "I have friends waiting for me."

I hear him walking away, the door shushing closed.

In the mirror I can see my socked feet. Behind them the man is working at a control panel, dancing in and out of the monitors' light.

Still, still, still, I think, but I can't stop squirming.

Elvis Costello is playing when the machine starts knocking. Then Wilco.

At some point, I'm taken out of the machine and a needle is stuck in my arm. My body warms. The top of my skull churns with heat lightning.

"Good pictures." The man's voice buzzes into the plastic tube. He says it every few minutes like a mantra.

I hear singing but do not know who it is. So many songs play into my locked-down head.

When I open my eyes again, the MRI is howling inside me.

6

Julie tiptoes around the room while I pretend to sleep. Standing in her panties, she stares out at the waning night, caresses her hamstrings. There's a pomegranate-sized bruise on her knee. She's wearing the blurred face people get when they think no one's around.

"Hey, baby. Good morning!" she whisper-sings. "Mornin', Al! I have to leave for the airport soon. Wake up, baby."

When she touches my cheek, I lunge and pull her back to bed, biting at her thighs. She shrieks and falls onto the mattress, laughing. "Quit! I need to leave! Let go of me! Let go!"

"Nope!" I laugh stonily. "Thinking you should stay. Gonna tie you up."

Giggling, she rolls her eyes and struggles out of my clasp.

I wedge a pillow under my chin and watch Julie

undress. After folding the T-shirt, she turns from the mirror, laughs, and shakes her head. When she throws the shirt, it curves and billows toward me like flames.

"You look so cute sleepy, squinting like that," she says, zipping up a suitcase. "I'll call as soon as I get there. Have fun in Florida with the guys. Don't forget to have a good time!" She bites my lip, paints a finger over my chin. "See you in a week. Gonna miss you, Al."

Julie kisses me again, and before I can ask if there might be a later flight, remind her that Dr. Floberg is calling soon, she turns off the sink light and rolls her luggage out.

The shadowy light is ulcerated, littered like fish scales across the room. Lying in bed, staring at the cobwebs, it's predictable and tedious—being alone suffocates me. I can't stand it. I remember being little, my mouth pulling away from my arm, thinking, *What's happening here? Who did this? What's going on?* after I'd just bitten the insides of my biceps. The red sickles *my* teeth made on *my* skin. *My* flesh wet with spit and blood. In high school, when the house was empty, I'd hit myself below the kneecaps with drumsticks until they swelled. "It's nothing." I'd tell anyone who asked about my limp or pointed out the yellowing. It didn't matter if no one saw them. I needed to feel it. To feel that pus-filled weight as I twirled my locker combination or jogged around the wrestling room.

The dorm's silence is bludgeoning so I turn everything on. The box fan, the stereo, each desk lamp, the

TV, the bulb above the sink, the jittery overhead fluo-rescent. I put my headphones on. On the floor, the minifridge door wags open, chilling my sockless feet. I gaze blankly at my sketchbook, then distend a fist of modeling clay, ball it back up, and smack it against the wall. I scrape it off and throw it at the ceiling. It hangs down like a bat. I boil a mug of water in the microwave, check my e-mail, and watch TV until I can't sit still any longer.

"Breakfast, Case. Come on, let's go!" I rattle his doorknob. "You gotta get up sometime, Golden." I shoulder-slam it a few times. The crook of my elbow is sore and violet where the needle went in last night. "You muthafucka!"

The hallway gets claustrophobic when I stop shout-ing, and my insides darken with the familiar craving for violence. I go slack and angry. "Fine, man. Enjoy your fucking fairy tale, you asshole." I throttle the door a final time, wishing he'd step into the hall so I could punch him for no good reason. "Come get me when you climb out of your sarcophagus."

II

1

"MORNIN', DR. FLOBERG." CRADLING THE PHONE, I TURN the stereo down. The crescent of chew drops from my lip into the bottle. "Yeah, sorry. How are ya, Doc?"

"Alex, you've had a brain hemorrhage."

"A what?"

"The MRI showed bleeding in your brain stem. A brain aneurysm."

"Are you sure? Really?"

"Additional tests need to be done."

"Wait. So . . ."

"You need to get to the hospital right away."

Not a soul is walking the concrete path outside my window.

"Alex, do you need help getting to the hospital?"

WHEN I CALL HOME, BOB SAYS THAT MA'S GONE TO WEATHerford to get groceries. My stepdad asks me to breathe, to slow down and tell him everything again. I babble, trying to make sense of what's going on, and as I unpack it for him—pooling blood, brain, some sort of stroke, the hospital and more tests—the truth drops through me like a rain of nails.

"The doctor said I have to get to the hospital so they can find out if it's still bleeding." Bob doesn't make a noise. The leaf-thickening branches are unmoving in the morning breeze.

"I'm going to go find your Ma, Al," Bob says, starting to cry. "We'll be up there as soon as we can. I love you."

During the summer, they live together in Oklahoma, fourteen hours away; the phone weighs a thousand pounds.

WHEN MY FATHER ANSWERS HE BRUSQUELY SAYS THAT they're running behind schedule, that they need to get a move on if they're going to catch their flight. He and Lindy are driving to Des Moines and then flying to Florida to watch me play. "We gotta scoot," he says, biting into an apple. "Can we take you out to dinner in Fort Myers? Something special?"

"Hold up a second, Pops," I say, shaking. "I'm not going."

"What? What do you mean you're not going? Did you get in trouble?"

I have to tell him the name of the hospital I'm going to twice. In the background, Lindy asks him what's wrong. After a minute, dumbfounded, he says to her, "Brain hemorrhage," like he just saw a solar eclipse.

"ALPHONSE, ALPHONSE!" CASEY SHOUTS WHEN I RUN INTO his room. He's rummaging through a closet, stacking T-shirts and balling up socks on the bed. "Thanks for waking me up this morning, buddy." He throws a sock ball off me, then slaps me five and goes back to piling jeans.

"I need another favor, Case." He looks up from the duffel. "The doctor just called. I need a ride to the hospital, man. I had a fucking brain hemorrhage."

"What?" He smiles, confused. "Come on, Al . . . You fucking with me?"

"No shit. He just told me." I thumb-point to the wall like the doctor's sitting in my room.

He stares at me for a second and then goes back to packing, meticulously sorting his laundry. "For real? That's fucked up."

"Yep. My brain stem or something."

"Shit, man. That's crazy." His hands go in and out of the bag like he's robbing a safe.

"Yeah, huh? Feels all sorts of wrong." I have never cried in front of someone my age, and I try to fight it, swallowing down the rock in my throat.

"You gonna die?" He looks out of the window, tries to laugh.

"Shit." I sputter. "Hope not." I can't fight it any

longer and I start to weep. "Casey, man. I don't know what the fuck is going on here." He knocks the pile of jeans to the floor and fumbles for his Parliaments.

"IT'LL BE OK, MAN," CASEY SAYS, PULLING UP TO THE HOSPItal curb. "I'll call and check on you in a bit." He sounds mystified. He didn't smoke one cigarette during the drive, just stared at the road. "Find out what the fuck's going on here."

"Casey, I don't know what to do, man. I don't know how to be sick."

"It will be cool, Al." He gives me a fist bump. "I'll come back in a minute."

The hospital's sliding door keeps opening and closing, but no one's going in or out.

"Shit, Al," he laughs distantly, looking straight ahead. "They'll probably turn you into the Bionic Woman."

I step into the sunshine before letting myself cry again.

STARING INTO THE SURGICAL LIGHTS WHILE THE NURSE shaves off my pubic hair, I plead silently—*Let the hard-on I'm getting be tremendous. Let me be OK, and this will be the greatest story I'll ever tell. My buddies will holler until bloody vodka shoots from their noses. When I tell Casey how the nurse gave me a blow job,*

he'll stand on his couch, cover his heart, and sing the
national anthem.

My breath catches when she nicks me with the razor
blade.

I'm splayed out on a hospital table and my brain is
bleeding. My brain is all fucked up, and I'm being
prepped for a cerebral angiography.

The nurse circles the plastic razor in the water, says,
"Oops, sorry about that," and starts again. Crinkling
lights. The razor blade snicks and burrs. "Just in case
the doctors can't use this artery," the nurse says. "I'm
going to have to shave the other side."

It feels like I'm underwater. Everything above me
looks blue.

A doctor slips the photo-catheter into an incision in
my right femoral artery. He threads it over a wire and
then winds it through my heart and up my carotid
artery. The medical team watches on a monitor, posi-
tioning the instrument. Before the contrast dye is
injected into my brain they tell me that I'll need to hold
my breath. "Now," one says, and dye floods the vessels
and veins in my head and it feels like I'm being broiled.

The blue room goes fuzzy and then turns dazzling
and prismatic. X-rays of my insides are magnified and
digitized on video screens: pictures of my pooling
blood surround us.

The doctors perform the contrast-dye-injecting pro-
cess again and again while I lie on the table. They
gather and point, murmuring. The room convulses and
beeps.

The doctors rub their masked chins, bodies willowing from side to side.

"ALL IN ALL," THE DOCTOR SAYS WHEN THEY WHEEL ME INTO the empty room, "things look pretty good. You have a vascular malformation in your brain stem, a pocket of blood in the pons. It started bleeding a while ago, weeks maybe, but luckily for you, it's stopped."

I nod at the doctor as he talks, but I'm so sleepy. There is no one here for me and I have no idea what his words mean. He says I need to get another MRI soon, but right now, the situation isn't dire. After Dr. Floberg talks to me about the brain lesion tomorrow, I can probably go home.

LINDY AND DAD ARE LEANING OVER MY HOSPITAL BED WHEN I wake that afternoon. She squeezes my forearm, says, "How you doing, old boy?" and smiles when I grin sleepily.

"Doing fine, I guess. How are you guys?"

With the shades open, the room is terribly bright, Easter-egg yellow, and it smells like green beans and witch hazel. There was no one in here when I fell asleep.

Dad shakes his head, chomping gum. He's dressed like we're going to the beach—khaki shorts and a sea green polo. His face is bright red. "What's going on here, Al?" His words are so soft I have to read his lips. "How do you feel?"

Happy

"I'm pretty good, Pops," I say, washing down bits of my chewed-up mouth with chugs of water, but it feels like crows pecked at me all day. "Nice to see you guys." I smile. "Thanks for coming."

THAT NIGHT, CASEY SKULKS INTO MY HOSPITAL ROOM LIKE a mime. He gently closes the door, shouts, "YO, LEMON!" and then whistles. "Looking good!"

"Eat me, Golden."

I ask him how he snuck into the hospital and he laughs nefariously, then whispers, *"Magic potion.* You look fucking crazy in here. How they treating you on the inside?"

He grins big, slaps my hand, and hugs me, then plops in the bedside chair while I tell him what's going on. "This sucks, Case." I flap the sheets. "Come on, man, look at this shit!"

"You gotta keep the dream alive, Al!"

"I'm fucking bored. Been sitting here all day. I need to get out of here. GET ME OUT!"

"Fuck it. You're good, right? You get to go home tomorrow? That's awesome. Fuck Florida, man. It sucks. Alligators and sunburn, you don't want to go there." Casey says he's jealous that I get to go home and relax all week, but I can't get excited. My face is numb and everything I look at is pixilated.

When I open my eyes again he's waiting for an answer to a question I didn't hear.

I repeat more of what the doctors told me, and he

nods and says, "Good stuff," but he understands even less of the medical-speak than me. "You gotta—"

"You know what the fucking brain stem does?" I interrupt. He looks at the muted TV. "Me either, man. Shit."

I feel bad for being an asshole, so after a few quiet minutes I pull my hospital gown up, fold the sheet down so it barely covers my dick, and uncover the white skin where my pubes used to be. "Pow!" I slap my belly. "This is what happens when something's wrong with your brain! Like a fucking baby, man. Smooth butter!"

Casey laughs as I go on, but halfway through my being-shaved story he's stopped smiling. Unnerved by his look, I forget the punch line. I feel so pathetic that I can't speak. A click and a wheeze kick through the hallway.

"Shit," I say. "Never mind. I was just being stupid."

He laughs awkwardly, "You're not fooling anyone, Lemon. Everyone will know you're just trying to make your tiny dick look bigger."

After Casey leaves, my teammates call from the pre–spring break party. Everyone slurs. They belch out words like goats. A stereo thumps in the background.

"Happy Lemon! Wish you were here, bad guy. Feel better, homey. See you soon, playboy."

"What is this thing? Yup? 'Ello? Whatever, man."

"Where you at, Happy? Get your punk ass down here."

"Hello? Who? Hey. Happy. What's going on, man? How you doing?"

"Happy, yo! Crazy shit, brah. Totally crazy!"

"Hope you feel better, Chet. Do it quick and come over."

I hold the receiver away from my ear as someone yells about a lap dance. "Fuckers," I say. "You fucking fuckers." I have no idea who I'm talking to. The line is a crush of hip-hop and *fuck-you-man*s.

MA AND BOB HAVE A GREASY VENEER WHEN THEY RUSH INTO my hospital room in the morning. They drove all night—up I-35 through Oklahoma, Kansas, Missouri, Iowa, and Minnesota—and under the fluorescent lights, they blink in slow motion and stare. The sterile walls gleam around us, and I'm ashamed I'm not comatose or dead.

"Ali. My baby." Ma says, hugging me. "My poor Ali." She's been crying, probably the whole drive. Tendrils of gray hair are lacquered down her cheeks. Her brawny hands weave a knobby shell over mine, fingers callused, furrowed with garden dirt. "Oh, Ali. What's going on? You OK?"

Ma's short, fireplug stocky, and Bob's tall and skinny behind her. He kneads her shoulders. They could be a weary *American Gothic*, if it had been painted by Thomas Hart Benton.

"Everything is good!" I smile wide, jubilantly telling them about the malformation in my brain stem. "The docs said everything looks good, that these bleeds are extremely rare. It's like winning the sweepstakes!" I laugh. "It'll never happen again. It's all good!"

Ma and Bob fidget, their throat-lumps like apples hanging over my bed.

Bob gives me a back-slappy hug when they drop me off on Sunday night, then folds into the passenger seat of the rust-doored Mazda GLC Sport and waits. I kiss Ma good-bye and limp toward the house as they back out of the driveway. Lindy waves from the window. Barking dogs click up and down on the kitchen floor. As the Mazda patters away, I can hear Ma grinding, shifting gears. The car horn bleeps.

My family agreed that I should spend the remainder of spring break at my father's acreage in Mason City, Iowa. After a week of rest, I'll return to Mac for the rest of the second semester. I'm going to take incompletes in two courses so I have time to concentrate on my health. I cannot play baseball this year.

"You need to rest up, Al," Dad says, cracking open a beer as he reads at the dining room table. "Relax while you're here. Let us take care of you for a while. It's R and R time!" he bellows. "Come on, son!" He wrangles my arm as I walk by.

Lindy is upstairs making the coats and bags and hats she sells at craft festivals. When the sewing machine thunders, my chair shakes. I lie back in the recliner and stare at the living room ceiling. The black Lab rests its cinder-block head in my lap. The basset hound cowers on the couch across the room, eyeing me.

"What movies do you want me to get tomorrow?" Dad stands in the doorway with his shirt off, gazing out the dark picture window. The house is on the outskirts of town, and at night, it's utterly black outside. "I have to show a couple of properties, but I was thinking we could go out for lunch. What do you say? Chinese?" The marine corps tattoo he got removed from his bicep is a four-inch flat-line scar. "The buffet sound good to you?"

"Sounds great. I'll be here."

Long after Dad and Lindy go to bed, I'm awake, still in the chair and still staring. The dogs trot to the kitchen and slurp from their water bowls. Bugs chirrup in the fields.

EACH TIME I CREAK DOWN THE STEPS FROM MY BEDROOM, a new CD or videotape is waiting for me on the table. When I open the fridge, my favorite snacks are stacked in the cold light. The three of us go to the Northwest Steakhouse or have pizzas delivered each night. There is ice cream and carrot cake and cases of Coke. Dad and Lindy spoil me rotten; it's been this way since I first started visiting him when I was in second grade. I'd eat and eat and eat, until my stomach turned inside out and I threw up. When I got back to Ma's after my once-a-month weekend, she'd fill the garbage with the

GI Joes and toy guns and the camouflage that Dad had bought me.

After a few days of walking around the house like something out of *One Flew over the Cuckoo's Nest*, I go outside. Sparrows pitch and flit away from the picture window. A couple on horseback clop back and forth on the road, waving when they see me in the tree shadows. Above the cornfield across North Carolina Avenue, the cement plant bulges the distant air with smoke. I say, "What's up?" to my reflection in the window glass. The TV plays *Braveheart* to the empty living room. Squirrels monster about in the birdseed Dad dumped out on the concrete slab above the septic tank. Wrapped in the crab apple tree's low limbs, I watch deer trot warily up to the salt lick. After throwing the fallen fruit at the neighbor's horses, I flop in the chiggery grass. The dogs sandpaper my face with their tongues. The sun shines. I laugh as the dogs nip and drop slobbery tennis balls and nuzzle my side.

2

WITHOUT WAKING JULIE, I SLIP OUT OF BED AND PUT MY workout clothes on in the dark. At her desk, I write a dozen love notes and scribble drawings that'll make her laugh. After hiding the Post-its around the room—folded in panties, stuck to a bar of soap—I whisper that I'll see her tonight and kiss her good-bye.

Campus is purple in the early morning light—picnic tables, an overturned chair in front of the Union, window frames, and the benches' stained wood. In front of each building, the blossoming flowers the gardeners have been planting have a metallic gloss. Leaves are bursting from the trees. In the stillness, a kid is sitting hunched on the steps of my dorm. He doesn't move when I wave. He looks like he's sleeping with his eyes open, a cigarette bent from his mouth.

When I get to the stadium the chain-link fence looks white-hot in the dawn air. I squeeze through a gap and walk across the track to the end zone of the football field, looking to make sure no one is in the stands before I ease myself down. Sunlight crawls through the grass.

I crouch in the dew and stretch and yawn and smile, listening to the city wake. I do push-ups, squeeze my fists, and pinch my skin. One by one, I flex the muscles in my legs and arms. I focus, trying to pluck each precise muscle fiber. I'm made of thousands of guitar strings.

On the track, I rehearse all of the doctor's orders. I stand on one foot. I hop. Again and again. I walk straight lines. I jog. I swerve across the lanes, my poor balance pulling me left and right, but I only slow when I'm going to fall.

When I lie back down, the day is already scorching. My vision bounces—it gets worse when I'm tired—but it's not as bad as it was at my dad's three weeks ago, so I watch birds careen across the sky. Clouds shred apart. A bee circles through the clover.

By the time I finish the exercises I've been doing each morning since I returned to Mac—everything everyone's been telling me I need to do to get better—the sun will have risen above the top of the stadium. On the other side of the bleachers, Snelling Avenue will be full and honking with morning's rush-hour cars. Drenched in sweat and shaking, I'll stop by Casey's room and grin, call him a sucker for having to go to class. *Incompletes my ass*, he'll laugh. *Fool, I got learnin' to get done!* He'll slap me five. *See you later,*

Happy

Al, you asshole! I'll walk around the art department and this afternoon I'll work out again. Tonight, Julie and I will watch a movie. Afterward, I'll listen to music and draw and read. I will not go out; I haven't partied since I was in the hospital.

And tomorrow, it will all happen again. The light will go from plum to sharp white and bright and my heartbeat will pound while the sun dries my sweat. Lying in the middle of the empty football field, the campus just beginning to stir, I'll feel myself getting better.

3

Two weeks later, I walk into Capital Neurology for my mid-April checkup. I had returned to Mac determined to pretend nothing had happened. When my buddies asked what happened, I brushed it off, acted like they were speaking in tongues. I'm doing my best to forget that there's something wrong; I've never worked harder at anything. But this is the first time I've had to talk about it to anyone other than Ma.

"You appear to be doing very well, Alex," Dr. Floberg says, shaking my hand. "Nice to see you." He taps my knee with a rubber mallet, looks at my eyes, and checks my limb strength, and then asks about my facial numbness and vertigo.

I grin and excitedly tell him how great things are going. "I think everything's getting better. Only notice it sometimes." I grin to cover my lie. "I feel good," I say, but really, I can't tell. My eyes bounce all the time—Dr. Floberg calls it nystagmus—and it makes the world flash and jump. Some days I think my cheek or arm or hand or leg is numb. I don't know anything anymore. I can't remember what it was like before.

"The lesion has probably been there forever. You were probably born with it," he says, "but it's extremely rare that they bleed. Many people have vascular malformations in their brains and live their entire lives without having any problems. Since it's no longer bleeding, there's no longer cause for alarm, and the likelihood of it bleeding again is very small." Dr. Floberg tells me that even though my most recent MRI looks good, I still need to be careful—I should be cognizant of activities that raise my blood pressure. He cautions against partying and sex. He says I can start working out a little harder, but I need to ease back into my life, and I'll have to get checkups once a year.

"The malformation is deep in your brain, in the pons, and the pons is very delicate. Very hard to get to," he says. "All of your body's hardware goes through the brain stem. But you're a fortunate young man. It could be much, much worse. If it had been a more severe bleed, your situation would be drastically different."

"So, like, what do I do?"

"I spoke to your mother on the phone and I told her the very same thing: I wouldn't do anything about it. Though there will always be a chance of the lesion bleeding again, the risk involved in any brain stem surgery is not worth it. At this point, in my opinion, the benefits of surgery do not outweigh the potential outcomes."

When he says *surgery* my stomach twists. My breath locks.

"The brain stem is crucial to life, and I wouldn't consider surgical excision right now. Wait and see what happens; another bleed is highly unlikely."

It feels like I'm being wishboned apart.

He asks more questions.

"I think I'm doing good," I chuckle slowly. "I think. Sometimes I just don't know." When he prods, I tell him about not sleeping well, that there are days I don't want to be around anyone, and I usually love everyone.

"Alex, what you've been through . . . what you're going through, is very serious. You need to be sure you're taking care of yourself. Right now, you need to think about your health—physically and emotionally. You're recovering wonderfully. Keep up the good work."

I wander around downtown St. Paul after the appointment. I do not feel like I'm *recovering wonderfully*. I'm not sure what I feel. I catch myself looking for my reflection in storefronts, trying to remember what it was like before. For hours I walk into open-doored businesses, and then, in a hardware store, I decide—I'm going to take whatever I can tonight. It's been too long. Things are good. I'm *recovering wonderfully* and I'm going to get fucked up. *Everything is just fine*, I tell myself, fondling bolts, fingertipping the points of power-saw blades.

4

I WIPE SWEAT FROM MY FOREHEAD, THEN PULL THE BATTING helmet down. I tighten my gloves and adjust my cup, and lift the bat to my shoulder, fluttering my fingers over the Easton's taped handle. Coach snags another ball from the bucket and I take a deep breath. He spits and grins. Behind him, beyond the batting cage net, last night's storm clouds are pulling apart, lashing to blue.

"Let's go, Chet." Coach looks to first base like he's checking a runner and then throws from the stretch, slide-stepping his front leg, loading his arm back, up, and behind him. His body twists, arm flashing through the air as he grunts. The baseball wings from his left hand, bulleting at my head.

When I look up after dropping the bat and ducking out of the way, he's laughing. "Good eye!" he shouts. "Thataway, Chester! A little chin music to keep you honest." He winks, spits again, and then grabs another ball.

I was furious when Coach told the team I wasn't going to play this year—first at myself, and then at everyone around me. Each game, I sit at the end of the bench in street clothes, hating my friends. They clap and yell "Turf monkey!" when someone trips on the Astroturf, and in the corner, I feel invisible. When the team isn't practicing, I go out to the field and hit off of batting tees. In the mornings I work out in the empty weight room, then throw into a net in the gym. I had to beg one of my teammates to soft-toss me balls at first, but Coach has made more time for me as the season's worn on. He's given me pointers on my swing, thrown tennis balls into the air to help me work my eyes, and finally, yesterday, he said he would stay after practice and throw me BP.

"All right, Coach! Come on!" I point the bat at him and smile. "Let's see what you got!"

The next pitch is spinning so hard a red dot stares out from the center of it. It drops right over the plate and I crush it, all sweet spot, right back at him. The ball rockets off the corner of the protective screen Coach is throwing behind and poofs out the batting cage net. He jumps back and smiles. "Whoa!"

For an hour, I smack each ball he zings at me, laughing when he says "Last one," and then throws it high and tight.

"All out!" he says, clapping his hands. "Pick 'em up." He throws the empty bucket toward the plate.

HAPPY

"You're getting too good, Chet. It'll be great to get your bat in the lineup next year. Glad you're going to play summer ball."

"I think everything's the same, Coach." I scamper around the Astroturf, pouching my shirt with baseballs. "I can't wait until next year."

But I haven't been able to stop thinking about what's wrong with me.

I started drinking on the bus after my neurology checkup two weeks ago, and by the time I stumbled down the steps at campus, everything *was* fine. Nothing was broken inside me. Now I'm pounding gin and whiskey and beers before games. Smoking joints in the port-a-potty. Popping pills. I don't want to be alone, but I can't stand the people around me, so I stay as fucked up as I can all the time. Saturday, I ate shrooms and sipped rum in my room, then sat in the corner of the dugout and watched the team play two. *No one can see me,* I thought, smiling. My teammates buzzed, swarming out of the dugout to line up at the plate to high-five Kawika after his homer. I could feel nothing at all inside me, but the baseball in my palm pulsed.

5

WE'RE DRINKING AND PLAYING POKER WHEN A STORY ABOUT pedophiles appears on the news. The cards are dealt, and for a minute my teammates watch TV. A beer cracks open. Someone *tsk-tsk*s. A bottle-cap pings off of the screen. I exhale and stare down at my hand like I can will myself better cards.

"Buncha fuckin' wackos," one of the guys laughs. "That shit is fucked."

"Awful shit, dude."

"You know, those poor fuckers will grow up to be sick bastards just like 'em."

"Yep. Monsters."

"Molesto the clown! Who wants a peek under the big top?"

"Shit makes me want to take a shower."

Everyone laughs.

"Oh, fuck this." I accordion my cards. "Another

bullshit deal." I don't really care that I have another terrible hand; I'm half in the bag and can hardly tell the diamonds from the hearts. "Let's go to the fucking party already."

"Shit, Happy—one more deal after this."

"Come on! One more, Chester the Molester!"

I fake-laugh and smile and focus on the blurred numbers, but I'm thinking about last week. Julie and I were watching the news in the dorm lounge while we waited for our tea water to boil. A reporter was knocking on the door of a sex offender, asking why he wouldn't speak to the camera. The students on the couch joked. Julie fingered the elastic on my shorts and I felt sick. The microwave beeped. Burgundy goop was splattered inside it like a lung had been cooked too long. When I dropped the tea in, water bubbled over the lips of the mugs. As Julie and I left, I heard one of them say, "Those kids are going to be fucked up."

"I'm done with this bullshit." I fold, tossing down my cards.

"No one likes a quitter, Happy."

"Eat a dick." Standing. I tip my head back and swig. I drink until it feels like someone's crumpling up my brain. Laughter shakes the room when the jokes start—it fills the cloistered space. Peter Pan and the paintings on the side of molester vans and Neverland Ranch and what kind of candy is best for picking up little boys. They make drinks for the party on Dayton—pack beers into backpacks and

pass around a tin of Skoal—and the jokes are endless. Dying of food poisoning because of eating nuts.
The Kiddie Fiddler and Grandpa's lap. I've heard
them thousands of times before. Everyone I know
says this bullshit. I do.

6

"CUT THAT SHIT OUT." BRAD YELLS THE NEXT NIGHT. He stands and slams the video game controller to the floor. "Will you two quit it!"

"Motherfucker. I'll kill you." I teeth-grind at Casey, my fingers pinching around his neck. I push him toward the windows, flipping the computer chair over, and then choke him. His face reddens and he coughs. "Muthafucker, with your big-ass mouth."

Casey grunts and turns away, loosening my grasp, and then swings his elbow wildly. Falling backward so it won't break my face, I let go of his throat. His elbow whooshes by my nose, and I lunge, shoving him against the wall and tearing at his throat again.

"Don't you ever take a swing at me!" I yell, crushing his windpipe. "Fuck you, Casey."

"FUCK YOU, AL," he croaks.

"YOU ASSHOLES! STOP IT! CUT IT OUT!" Brad

says, wrenching us apart. "NOW NOW NOW!" He pushes me back. Without taking his eyes off of me, Casey slowly rights the chair. Heaving, he stands in front of the TV.

"Enough. Jesus Christ." Brad looks back and forth between us. "You guys cool?"

"The fuck is your problem, Al?" Casey stares, fists clenched in front of him. "Huh? The fuck, man? Asshole."

Walking around campus by myself, I can't remember how the fight started. I don't know what Casey said. I don't know if he said anything at all. I just opened my eyes and my fingers were squeezing his throat.

7

Julie's roommate is gone for the night but we still whisper, siphoning out of our clothes. Her bedspread makes us smolder slick yellow in the dark. She's gorgeous, gulping as I kiss down her neck and chest and navel. I nibble the small cups above her collarbones and she moans. I lick down her belly, run my teeth over her hip bones until she laughs and pulls me up by my hair. She bites my mouth, then looks in my eyes and grabs my dick, says she wants me.

She plays with my penis but it makes me cringe. She tugs and whispers and I can't get an erection. I'm numb when she says she *needs* me inside her. She tongues my ear, jerking faster, but nothing happens.

I grapple her hand away from my body and pin it to the sheets. I'm humiliated, angry at her because I can't get wood. I kiss her mouth roughly and push my fingers into her, softly at first, and then harder and harder.

85

Long after we're finished and Julie is asleep, I creep out of bed and sit at the desk, naked and cold and pissed. The curtains flutter in the quiet like someone's standing behind them.

A few weeks after we started dating I realized that Julie is the first woman I've had sex with while I was sober. Before her, each time I was fucked up. When we make love, I tell Julie that it was wonderful, the best ever, better than all those other girls. And it's true. But if I haven't been partying, there are times I can't stand being touched and others when I can't fuck no matter how much I want to.

I'm standing in front of the window when I open my eyes. I don't remember getting up from the desk, blowing out the candles, and walking to the other side of the room. A procession of shadows on the lawn. Swabbed in moonlight, my naked body looks like an anatomy model—corded veins and fibery slats of muscle. A wagon wheel of organs. A barely beating heart.

I blink and blink and blink, but the little boy appears each time I close my eyes.

Rain again, the little boy thinks as he stares out the second-story window. No. No. No. *Rain again, I* think, as *I* stare out of the second-story window. No. Rain again. No. I am the little boy. I slowly unbutton my shirt and it falls to the floor. There is no sound coming from the rooms below. What had been a torrential downpour outside is now a hazy Oregon mist. The slick shingles on the roof outside look like the scales of a mythical beast. *We are inside the monster,* I think, *but it is OK.* I am almost five, and I want to know why my hair, which had been white-blond, is now almost completely brown. I flex my hand against the glass. I'm completely naked. My paleness flushes in the darkened bedroom. As much as I like living with my aunt's family, I think about when I'll get to return home to live with Ma.

When the giant hand grabs me, my wrist is twisted until I can no longer look through the rain-beaded glass. My head is wrenched. My body flinches. An erect penis smacks me in the face. The hard flesh jabs me in the lips, punching it like my own small fist. A wetness streaks down my cheek. I wonder why my cousin's penis is so big compared to mine. Why there is so much hair curling around the giant stick. How my cousin moves so silently through the darkness.

After staring out into the bright light of the window, I cannot see anything in the dark room. There is a persistent pushing against my lips. I cannot hear what my cousin is yelling at me, but, over the months, the mean heat radiating off his body is a language I have come to understand.

My cousin is angry; he flashes teeth. I close my eyes. The teenager is twice my size, towering over me. He had locked the door behind me with one hand and unzipped his jeans and pulled out his penis with the other. His penis grew and stiffened each time he yanked it. I thought it might grow forever. He lay back in the bed and his penis stood straight in the air. Next to him, the knife rested on a pillow. He grinned, spitting on his palm and stroking his penis. I looked toward the window.

After my mouth is used, he lifts the bright blade into the dark air. The knife is the only thing that is allowed to glow in the bedroom. He rolls the sharp light in his hand and then presses the tip into my scrawny chest. My cousin smiles and threatens to kill the people I love if I tell anyone about what happens in this room.

My face is covered by a gag of fingers, and I'm swung around again. I'm dizzy. Smacked. I wish he'd believe me when I promise not to tell. I have understood for a long time now. All summer I've known that this is OK, but my cousin thinks I'm a liar. He breathes like he's choking, then exhales steam. But since the first time the door was locked behind me, I know that this is the way it happens. It is normal for him to moan and slam me around the bedroom.

There are times, when everything is numb and there's no pain, that I like what happens in the dark room. I want to be touched. I do what my cousin orders me to so he'll be nice. I know that he is doing these same things with my best friend, his five-year-old sister.

8

"WE COOL, MAN?" I ASK CASEY AS THE LIGHTER FLICKS. We've been walking around campus, not talking to each other for an hour, and finally, he sat in the grass in front of the Union. I roll to my back, and the Vicodin and gin I'd been putting down when he knocked sloshes. "You hear me, Case?" I sit up, and a warm tide rises into my throat. It's taken me a week to say anything about our fight. "Are we cool, man?"

He stares, eyes wire-thin, and then watches some girls walking toward the library.

"Are *you* cool?" He vents smoke out of his nose. "Al?" Cherries fall through the dark when he taps his finger against the P-funk. "Yo, Al."

"Yeah, Case . . . I'm . . ." I can't tell him I'm sorry, because I'm not. "I'm cool, man, of course. So we're cool, right?"

He half utters, stops, and then nods slowly. "Yeah. We cool."

"Good, man. 'Cause the docs filled me with new blood! The good shit this time," I laugh. "Damn, son! I'm perfect. Feeling nice right about now!"

"Shit, man," he says, finally smiling, "you been an asshole. They put asshole blood in you. You really feeling OK, or you fuckin' with me?"

"All that shit is done and gone." I flip him off and shake my head. "And you, too, you're my favorite asshole anyways."

"Whatever, Lemon, you douche."

It's far past midnight, and the trickle of students shuffling back to the dorms has stopped. A warm wind thrushes through the trees.

"Feeling excellent, man!" I point at him, then jab his chest. He fakes a punch, and I flinch.

"Ho, ho, ho, bitch." Casey takes a drag; the cigarette is a tiny red eye, blazing in the dark.

"Fuck you," I grin. "I'll make a hookah out of your skull. Gimme one of those."

"You're a funny man, Lemon." Casey tosses me the pack and looks off. Headlights cruise by on Grand. On the other side of the street kids run and yell across the open lawn. "Make me shit my shorts I laugh so hard."

"I'll choke you out and leave you on the steps of the Union." I shove him again, softer this time.

"You gonna bring it?" He howls. "Bring that shit! Bring out the gimp!"

Happy

"Watch yourself, Golden." I smoke, ash blows into the night, and then we both laugh.

"For real, Al." In the light his face softens. "It's great, man. You feeling good and shit."

For a month I did exactly what the doctors wanted me to do, and now I'm getting back into my old life, but it feels like I'm sinking, like I'm trying to breast-stroke through oatmeal. I don't sleep and I'm angrier than I've ever been. Lying all of the time, for no good reason. Some mornings I wake and find money or drugs in my jeans and none of it's mine. It takes days for me to remember stealing it.

"I've never been better, Case. I'm the goods." I laugh, but since I was in the hospital I've been losing my mind.

9

A BLADE OF LIGHT STRETCHES BELOW THE DOOR. PIPES shudder while I turn through the sheets. I get out of bed and stare blankly at the spring leaves.

All year Brad and I have stayed up laughing at *Loveline*, the sex-talk radio show that's hosted by a comedian and a doctor. Cackling in the dark, trading barbs while callers talk about abuse and rape and sexual perversions. The doctor is attentive to each caller—the people with real problems, even those who give shout-outs and talk about their penis piercings. He gives advice while the comedian laughs.

It's hilarious when Brad's around, but he's never in the room anymore. He always stays at his girl-friend's.

Every time I've closed my eyes the last month, the little boy has appeared. I have appeared. But now, when I turn from the window, the little boy is standing in my room. He's pale, scarecrowish, and smiling.

In the dark, voices mutter to me all night. They say I'm a monster—that it is only a matter of time. I will do terrible things because that's what little molested boys do when they grow up.

10

"You!" CASEY SLAMS INTO MY ROOM. HE'S IN A RAGGEDY wife-beater and long basketball shorts. His hair is flattened on one side and his eyes are sleep-puffed. "Dirty, dirty you!" He dangles a flip-flop from his foot, then flings it across the room at me.

"Hey, Case," I grin up from a book. It falls from my lap when I toss the sandal back. "Good morning to you, too. My bestest o' pals."

"You fucking guy. Fuck you, you!" He finger-jabs at me each time he says *you*, and shakes his head. "Can't believe you."

"Chill, asshole. What did I do?" My desk is spotless. Class notebooks arranged alphabetically. Pens, markers, in a Macalester mug. A list of assignments is tacked to the wall beneath the Chet Lemon baseball card. Machiavelli and *The Collected Poems of Emily Dickinson* are stacked on top of xeroxed poli-sci essays. It's less than four weeks until summer, the end of my freshman year.

"Fucking Lemon."

"What's up, man? What's wrong?" I've been up for three days straight and my blood is still humming. The drugs are stuffed in a plastic shark in a drawer with another souvenir of my youth—a steel Mickey Mouse spoon that Ma sent in a care package.

Casey turns and pulls his shirt up. His back is cross-hatched with red carvings, scratches from his shoulders to his ass crack.

"Oh shit, Casey!" I laugh because I know who did it. "Oh damn, you been got!"

After a party this fall Macey staggered back to campus with me. When Casey knocked on the dead-bolted door, her black panties were hanging over the side of my desk. The runny eye shadow made her look enraged. I pulled a fist of her hair and her neck stretched back and she yowled, legs snaked around me, fingernails slicing my chest.

"I can hear you in there, you fucker," Casey yelled as Macey and I slammed together. "Hey, Al! I hear youuuuuuuuuu!" I ground my teeth and tried to cover Macey's mouth but she wouldn't stop. She bit and dug and moaned while Casey hammered on the door. "Al. You bastard. I hear you, I hear you, I hear you." Casey chanted in the hall.

In the bathroom the next morning Casey asked which girl it was but I said it was privileged information. "Nothing happened, Case. Don't know what you're talking about." I smiled. "Must have been Brad."

"She was fuckin' loud, Al. Come on, tell me. Who? Which one?"

"Crazy night. Long night," I said, taking my shirt off to shower.

"Shit, man. You fuck a jellyfish last night?" I turned so he could see the long ones on my back.

"You fucker," Casey says, clapping the sandal against the bedpost. "You should have told me. As soon as her nails got me, I knew. Fuck, man, I knew! I couldn't stop thinking that you'd been there first. Didn't know if I was going to come or puke."

"Ha! Them's the breaks, Case. Hey, you wanna get some breakfast?"

"Not sure about omelets. I feel sick." He smiles when he says it. "I need to find a way to boil my entire fucking body."

"It is what it is, man. I'm always better than you, Golden. I'm fucking two steps ahead of you."

"Lemon, you bullshit artist."

"It's hard, Casey, you know, having all this love to give!" I growl and claw my hand through the air.

11

Holy shit—THE DOCTOR IS PALMING MY DICK IN A GLOVED hand like he's going to guess its weight. He twists it down like it's taffy, puzzles over the stretched flesh. When he speaks I look directly into his eyes. He looks surprised that the penis he's holding is attached to someone. When the room quiets, I stare at my dick. Holy holy shit. My dick is in his hand.

"OK, then," he says, "this will only take a second. I'll come check on you in a little while. You should know right away if it's going to give you an erection." He holds my dick casually, like a pocket watch.

The doctor spent less than five minutes talking to me; the motherfucker hardly asked anything. "There's a pill in the works, but injection is the most reliable method right now," he said, before asking me to take my shorts off and cover my genitals with a paper cloth.

"The solution needs to be injected into one of the

sides of the penis to work. Make sure it's not in a vein," he says, pushing the needle in my dick. "That's not good at all. It can cause severe pain." He doesn't look up. "Do you think you can do this?"

I try to say yes, but my mouth is a big O of hurt. When I look at my dick again, there's still a needle in it. I stare at the doctor—he's got my dick in one hand, a syringe in the other. He's not even talking to me; he's talking to my dick like it's his pet, my dick, the one with a needle ramming it.

"I'll check on you in a little bit," he says. "If it's something you are interested in, I'll write you a pre-scription." The syringe drops to the tray. The bulbs are all on, but the room has a dim, cheap fluorescence. When he closes the door, the rickety walls tremble.

I have to wait in Casey's Blazer in front of the phar-macy because I still have a boner. I pitter the steering wheel with one hand and shove the other down my shorts and Morse-code the needle hole. Unfuckingbe-lievable. For a half hour I think of what I'm going to buy to make my buddies believe I went shopping. New shoes, new jeans, a stack of new CDs—I've lost my shit—anything to hide the package of needles in. Julie and I are going to Taste of Thailand; I need to get a dozen yellow roses.

12

"It's your Maaaaaa!" the phone message trills. "Ma. Ma. Ma. Ma. Ma." She sounds like a kick drum. "Call me, call me, call me, call me. Al! Call me. Caaaaaaaalll meeeeeeeeee!" The line quiets, and she sighs into the phone. "Why don't you ever call your Ma?" she asks mournfully. She waits a second, titters, and then hangs up. The next message was recorded ten minutes later. "Call me back. Call your Ma back. Back. Now. Back." She sets the phone down and then sings and plays accordion until the message ends. "Rescued six plants from the city dump today . . . ," the message from an hour later begins. She talks for minutes before the line starts beeping. "Gotta go. Al, gotta go! No more minutes on the calling card. I love you and worry about you. So call me. Call your Ma!" Yesterday she left the Rascals' "A Beautiful Morning" on the answering machine and said "Ma!" right as the song finished.

99

"Yo yo Ma!" I shout when she answers. "What's happening?"

"'Bout time you called me back, sonny boy! What took so long?"

"College is busy. Stuff. Doing lots of stuff."

"Well, how're you, Tiny?"

I tell her that Dr. Floberg thinks we should go to the Mayo Clinic sometime this summer to talk to a neuro-surgeon, to get more opinions.

"You want me to work on it? I'll start working on it," she says. "Don't worry about it." I hear dishes splashing in the sink. "I'll take care of it. So you're doing all right?"

"Yeah, Ma. Things are great here."

"You're taking it easy? No lifting weights hard? Treating yourself good?"

"Yeah."

"You sure?"

"Yep."

"Alllliiiiiii, you sure? You sound like something's up."

"Nothing, Ma. Really."

"You want to see that homeopath? You're eating good food, right? Staying away from caffeine and sugar? You should see one of the homeopaths up there. I know some good ones. Help you relax."

"Sure, Ma. Yeah, I'll—"

"You sure you're OK?

"Ma!" I snap, and it quiets. "It's just, you know, lately I don't want to be around anyone." She doesn't say a word. "Sometimes I don't want to be touched." I surprise myself.

I hem and haw while she asks questions, but Ma's no-bullshit. When she found out about the molestation, and the shit went down with the police and family services, she told her brothers and sisters that they could visit us on her terms. Our house. Her rules. And after that, we hardly ever saw them. When I was fourteen she gave me a drawing she wanted me to consider before having unprotected sex. She explained how if I had sex with a person who had sex with ten people who each had sex with seven people I was having sex with every single person in town. The stick figures rotated around her drawing of me like dozens of sharp stars.

Instead of hanging up when she asks "Like erections?" I choke out a "Yep."

She asks if I want to see someone but doesn't wait for an answer. She lists homeopaths I should make appointments with, the remedies I need to take, and what I should be doing to ensure the health of my adrenal glands. "I'll send you some more vitamins," she says. "E-mail you some articles about stress."

"Ma, I'm fine," I say when she finally stops talking. "Just wanted to say hi. See how you are. It's nothing really. I'm just off some days. Stressed out."

"I know you don't like to be told what to do, but you should listen to me. You should—"

"Fuck, Ma. Don't worry about me so much." My voice is cruel and she goes completely silent. "I gotta boogie, Ma." My cheeks burn. I start to tell her that I'm meeting with a study group but she's already hung up.

THE FIRST THREE TIMES THE SYRINGES FROM THE STRIP-MALL doctor worked, but right now, I'm way too sober. I take another chug, listen to make sure no one's in the bathroom. The bottle echoes when I set it on the shower tiles. My dick is frigid, shrinking and bobbing like it's trying to suck back into me. The needle shakes. I'd have to drop out of school if anyone found out I was shooting my dick up.

When I hear someone in the hall I kick the bottle over and beer glugs out, rivering down the drain. A guy picks up the phone in the hallway outside; it's one of the twins from California but I can't tell which. Each drip from the leaky showerhead sounds like a backfiring engine. I hold my breath and, trembling, push the needle into my dick.

A dot of red blood appears where I pull the needle out. It bubbles into a crimson marble and then paints down my penis and drops. I lean against the wall because I'm going to pass out. The blood plops and spreads in the tiled grooves.

I've lost my fucking mind.

I wipe my eyes, wrap a towel around my waist, and then fold the pharmacy bag into a fistful of paper towels. I stuff all of the needles to the very bottom of the trash.

13

Baying. I bounce on the air mattress. My heart flops up and down like a Ziploc bag of ground beef. Casey waves the giant toy boxing gloves on the other side of the game ring, urging me on. "Come get some, asshole!" he shouts, and then I'm floating in the air. I see the art department. The blue blue sky. My insides sink when I land. Casey's making faces and hissing. "Going to snuff you out, Lemon." He twirls the gloves like Muhammad Ali. "Here comes my Springfest special."

"Die, bitch!" I burble. The big gloves are so heavy I can only raise one, but I punch him flush in the nose and he staggers backward. I crash into him and we fall, laughing uncontrollably. Casey rolls and hops up, but I can't move. Everything is hilarious and I'm so fucking tired.

He pounds on me when I totter up but it's like getting mugged by a waterbed. "EEEEEEEE!" He screams and laughs and jumps, and then tackles me. My belly hurts so bad from laughing I just tumble and cover my face. After whacking me in the head a few times, he retreats to his corner, but as soon as I'm up, he bounds forward, beating his chest and screaming, "OOOAAAOOAA!"

I spring as high as I can and load up, punching as he swings. The glove smacks the top of his head when I come down and he crumples.

The clown-colored world is spinning when we roll out of the ring and stand up on the softball field. I fall into the dirt. Laughing, Casey picks up our drinks. He rights me, slaps my cheek hard, and hands me a cup. It's not even noon, but the softball field, fenced in for Springfest, our annual all-campus party, is covered with students. A girl in a swimsuit and skirt walks by blowing bubbles. On the hill behind home plate people are smoking and laughing and singing. Zoot suits and costumes and kids helping each other walk. A knight in armor made of beer cans. A few spaced-out dancers are waving their arms in front of the stage, where a guy in a dress taps his guitar with a spoon. The beer garden is packed, and an airhorn keeps blowing. It smells bummy and sweet and sour.

"Did you see me box Megan?" Casey asks as we try to find Art, a friend of ours who's passing joints out. "I'm fucking unstoppable. A phenom."

I try to say that Megan is smaller than him, but it sounds like I'm throat-singing.

"Al, you're speaking Lemonese, man. What the fuck?"

I WAKE IN THE DARK TO THE HUSHING DRIZZLE OF RAIN. At least I'm in my bed this time. I roll onto the slummed-out floor and hold my head.

Mud is streaked over the walkways in front of my dorm. The black and blue city light makes it seem like I'm floating over the ocean bottom. Thousands of shoe tracks circle the concrete around me. Dance steps. Smashed bugs. I stumble down the sidewalk to Shaw Field, but Springfest is over. The stage and games and beer garden are closed.

Casey is smoking with a group of our friends, talking about going down to the Mississippi and eating more shrooms. I groan and laugh and slobber down my chin until he looks.

"You have a nice sleep there, buddy?" Casey stares at the tip of his cigarette. His eyes are all fucked up, wavering blank and huge.

"Yikes." I try to smile. "A power nap."

It's impossible to see anyone's face except when the lighter flicks, and for a while, I can't talk or move. A drink is pressed into my hands, a pipe makes the rounds, and soon, the darkness fades. A guy swims in the mucky grass, crawling his arms and kicking. I look up to point it out to Casey, but he's gone.

"I'm gonna live on a catamaran," I laugh to whoever is sitting near me, "when we're done with this place." I point my cigarette around campus. No one has a face anymore; they're all wearing creosote masks. "Might just vanish. You'll get my letters from the fucking circus, man. Like the Unabomber, you bitches!" I laugh and yell and spill down my face, then kiss the girl next to me. Closing my eyes, I lay back as she slides onto me.

"Fuckin' gotta love it," a voice says in the misting dark.

All of us cough frozenly when we get up to leave, laughing and packing our backpacks. The rain's picked up, spines of light diagonal down from the sky.

"It's going to be a beautiful night, Happy!"

"Always is," I mumble.

July 1997

MA'S HAIR STAIRCASES OVER THE HEADREST, A WHITE BLAZE
in the wind. Growing up, strands of it were everywhere
and it was stronger than rebar. During Friday night
football games, I'd be tying my cleats in the huddle
and see a gray rope of it tangled in my laces, and it
would cling to me until I had time to scissor it off at
halftime.

Ma rolls the window down for fresh air again, but a
minute later she's too hot and seals the car up. Blasts
the air-conditioning. The pressure change makes me
stretch my jaw and pop my ears. She does it four times
in ten minutes. Each time I catch her eye in the rear-
view, I try to look excited, but the car is a sauna. My
head's been throbbing since we picked Julie up at the
airport.

Julie turns in the passenger's seat and smiles when I roll my eyes. I'm in the backseat on the driver's side, so I can read her face. She's the first girlfriend Ma's ever spent time with.

Ma rolls the window down again. Rolls it back up.

"Stop it," I say harshly. She'll do it all the way to the Mayo Clinic if I don't.

"What?" She mouths *"TONE"* silently into the rear-view mirror.

"The window thing, Ma. Please?"

"Sure, Al." She fiddles with the AC knob and then asks, "That OK?" Her eyes stare palely at the road.

"Yeah, Ma. Good, thanks." I fake-smile, but her glance unspools me so I look at the streaking fields. They are seas of green, eddying with sunshine. In the west, the clouds are gunmetal bluffs.

I'M IN SECOND GRADE. I PEDAL TOWARD THE BIKE RAMP AS three older boys stand on the top steps of an entrance to the school, urging me on. They chant. The street blurs. After the bike rockets into the air, I turn to smile, to make sure they see how high I'm soaring, but the bullies' pants are unzipped, and they're laughing, drenching me in spit and pee. When I tell Ma why I am soaked, she tears off on her bicycle, crying and swearing she's going to get them. The afternoon darkens, and I wait on the porch for her to come back. All night, she fingerlocks her mug. Her temples pulse. Her face fumes.

MA'S NEVER OWNED A BRAND-NEW CAR BEFORE THIS ONE; she'd been driving the last one, the Mazda, since I was in third grade. When my friends asked what the rotary phone on the dashboard was for, she'd tap the big old thing and whisper, "It calls the moon."

I know she and Bob bought the Escort in case they need to drive up to Minnesota more. She said she cleaned it but I'm kicking rocks and jugs of water, a bag of empty Mendota Springs bottles. Plant catalogues are stacked on sketchbooks and flyers for auctions and Dick Blick ads. The arm of a doll slides around on top of a stack of books. Cassette tapes thunk on the floor.

With the hatchback packed with bags, it feels like we're moving again; it seemed like Ma and I did it every few years. The Technics record player and speakers came to each city. Our favorite mismatched cups filled with new-tasting water, and a box of baking soda sat on the new bathroom sink. We always lived on the fringes and I coveted what my friends had—instead of snacking on Twinkies, when no one was looking, I'd nibble leftover pancakes. A slice of lemon in water instead of Pepsi. She'd make me a new birthday crown each year, and underneath my breakfast plate, a one-dollar bill was tucked into a book. In each town, I'd make friends with a crowd of faces but eventually leave and never speak to them again.

Ma won't stop telling Julie about me—how I mimicked Japanese women in Hawaii supermarkets and hunted frogs with Rito, our elderly Filipino landlord. The Mohawk I had in high school. How, after growing my hair out, my dyed braids stained my football helmet green. But no matter how macho I acted, I came home each night to eat with her.

When Ma speaks, I watch Julie's reaction, afraid, waiting for her face to droop with recognition. For her to frown disgustedly, knowing about all the nights I stared at Ma from the doorway of my room, quietly sobbing. The hours I watched Ma read on the Salvation Army couch, panicked that she'd be gone if I fell asleep, scared that if I stopped watching her, she'd die.

"He was so sweet to everyone," Ma says, smiling. Her cheeks sponge with color as she drives, talking about how considerate and caring I've always been. "When I was in college my friends loved that he was around all the time. He's always loved everyone. My beautiful baby."

"He still does," Julie says. She smiles at me and I squirm. I shake my head and mouth *"You're beautiful"* and *"It's all bullshit."* I can't shake the feeling that Julie can see the real me now. The weakling. The pussy.

THE NEUROLOGIST SETTLES ON A STOOL IN FRONT OF ME while I talk. A mob of younger doctors and assistants stand behind him. When the neurologist starts talking in monotone, one of them checks his hair in the glass cabinet above me. Ma writes everything down. The

neurologist does what all the other doctors have done;
he checks my eyes, my strength, and my reflexes, then
gives me his impression of my medical situation.

"After looking at your newest MRI, it's most likely a
cavernoma, but I wouldn't rule out an AVM." He
sounds bored and goes on flatly. "Recent studies have
shown that your type of brain stem malformation car-
ries a higher risk of recurrent hemorrhaging."

Ma asks questions, and the doctor stares at me when
he answers. I try to drift away while they talk, but
Ma's eyes are hard and sad.

IT'S JULY; I JUST FINISHED NINTH GRADE. THE SUN IS A
blinding stupor off of the Iowa River when Ma pulls up
next to me at the stop sign. "Get the fuck home. Now,"
she says, looking through me. "You were supposed to
be home at eleven. Last night." Her eyes are red.
"Hours. I've been looking for you for hours. You're
grounded. Until I say you can leave. Until tenth grade.
Fuck. Maybe Christmas." I walk my bike up Bliss Boulevard, hoping I don't smell like booze or weed. She
trails a few yards behind me as I sort through which
lies I'm going to tell.

"THERE'S PROBABLY A FIVE PERCENT CHANCE OF IT HAPPEN-
ing again, maybe a bit more," the neurologist says.

Ma nods and scribbles in the notebook and asks a
question. It takes everything I have to listen. Each time

Ma speaks I'm startled. I'm nineteen, and I don't know what to say during my appointments so she has to come with me.

"We learn more about the brain every day," he says. "So these numbers might change, but we know your malformation is in a highly eloquent area. That is very serious." I look up and he says it again, "A highly eloquent area," lets the words sink in, and then continues. "It is more likely to bleed again where your lesion is, but really, chances are it will never happen again."

"Are there lifestyle issues we should be thinking about?" Ma asks.

I'm dizzy, my head jerking back and forth.

"He can do what he wants to do," he answers dryly. "There isn't any clinical evidence to say one way or another why these bleeds happen, but you"—he looks at me hard—"should be aware of any hypothetical risks your choices in activities might have. If you feel like you can continue playing baseball, I would play another position. Catching puts you at a very high risk of head trauma. You cannot do that."

"What would you recommend?" Ma asks.

"I wouldn't do anything about it right now. I'd wait and see what happens. In truth," he says, "it could have been much worse. The malformation is no longer bleeding. You're in excellent shape and you might keep getting better. If it happens again, even though it's in a highly eloquent area, chances are it won't be catastrophic."

The force of Ma's note-taking whitens her knuckles.

"But I need to make sure I'm very clear. Let me reiterate. There's always a possibility of it bleeding again. The likelihood is very small, but you must remember that.",

Ma stares, then asks what our options are.

"Of course, there are things you might want to consider. There's surgical excision and Gamma Knife radiosurgery, but radiation hasn't yet been effective on cavernomas. And since the malformation is in a highly eloquent area, any type of surgery would be very risky. The potential benefits have to be weighed against what harm might result from the surgery. The brain stem is critical to your life."

The room quiets, hot and dark. The neurologist scratches his head, and I want to stick a pen in his eye.

"Besides," he says, pointing to a diagram of a brain, "I don't know many neurosurgeons who would want to try to get this one. That," he says, stabbing the pen tip to the spot of blood in my brain before he slips it in the breast pocket of his lab coat and turns, "is some very pricey real estate."

"Good news," Ma says, wrapping an arm around my waist while we walk. "Yeah, yeah, good news! But, man, Ali, that hospital shit is exhausting! Don't know how you do it!"

"Yuck." I stick out my tongue and then smile, relieved to be outside and close to her and Julie. "For sure. Did you see that asshole doctor checking out his hair? Fuck that guy!"

Julie laughs and pinches my shoulder.

Ma is giddy, says, "No more hemmies for us!" Her face is tired but she's grinning now that we're in the parking lot. She's started saying *hemmie* instead of *hemorrhage*; I smile, but it makes me think I've got brain hemorrhoids. "Oh, Tiny," Ma says. "We're done with that shit! Love you, Ali."

I kiss the top of her gray head as she fidgets away.

"Thanks for coming, Jules." I sail my fingers across her butt. "Thank you so much."

"It's wonderful news!" Julie says after Ma sinks into the driver's seat. We stand next to the Escort as the engine starts, kissing so Ma won't see.

But the car fills with a waterlogged silence when we're on the highway. I watch the pavement out the rear window, trying harder, with each passing mile, not to weep. *Highly eloquent area.* When I close my eyes I see the neurologist's exam room, and it's overpowering with plastic models of brains. They line and stack the shelves like championship basketballs. There are posters of lungs, charts and diagrams of the heart, but always, and everywhere, more brains. Other doctors, assistants, stand behind the neurologist, shifting their weight, looking at their watches. The room blacks out and my MRIs, pictures of my bleeding brain, mural the walls.

An hour later, still looking out the rear window, I realize that our lane doesn't have a crack down its center. The Escort curves to the other side of the highway and there the dark line is—following the car. I wait a half hour to say anything.

"What'd you say?" Ma turns down NPR, looks at me in the rearview, and points her hand like the pope. "'S'up with you back there, Ali?"

Julie looks over her shoulder sleepily.

"Shit, shit, shit," Ma says when I point out the crack. "Fuuuuuuuuuck."

"It's been back there for a while. An hour or so," I say. "I think we're leaking something."

Ma exhales long and strained, hand veins rising from her skin. She looks into the mirrors before changing lanes but almost sideswipes an SUV.

Julie is wide awake now, but she doesn't say a word.

"Everything's fine," Ma says. "Fine, fine, fine." She messes with the radio buttons, then plows a comb through her hair. She pulls a handful of snarled white from the teeth and then holds her hand out of the window. The scribble of hair zooms past me.

On my belly under the Escort, the dripping tube looks like an IV. I dip my fingers into the puddle, but the gas smell is obvious. Semi wheels hurl by on the interstate and I take as long as I can, wondering if it might be possible to climb into the undercarriage and never come out.

"Smells like gas," I huff matter-of-factly.

Ma says that this shit isn't supposed to happen to new cars.

It's 1996, the summer before I leave for college. Ma and Bob and I are driving to St. Louis, and our car's caught between trailer trucks in a deluge. The wind-shield streaks black, like we've plunged into a lake, and time, spectacularly, stops.

Ma says, "Ooooooooooooh, oh no, ooooooooooh, SSSHHHHHHIIIIIIIIIIT," hunching over the wheel as the trucks rumble by. A whole day passes before the wipers swing back to life. The highway appears through the whorls.

When the semis are a half mile ahead of us, Ma relaxes, singing out "Shittin' be gettin'" and smacking Bob's thigh. "Sooner or later," she says, turning down the stereo, "a steel pipe is going to fly off one of those fuckers and spear me to the seat. *Shooosh. Smack.*" She flicks her fingers into tiny explosions and says that it'll leave us ruined.

"Ma." I shake my head.

"It's true." She smiles. "I am the funniest one in the family. I am."

"Don't talk like that, Ma."

Bob ignores her. He rebuckles his seat belt, shifts, adjusts his lumbar pillow.

"Without me you guys wouldn't have any fun. Life without me would be boring."

"Ma. Come on. Why do you always say shit like this?"

"You will never have fun again," she says sullenly. "BORING!"

"Cut it out, Ma."

She lets the car go quiet, playing us.

"If I'm barely hanging on, or the fuckers are keeping me alive, you have to pull the plug. Don't let them keep me going. Do you hear me? Rub a dub, pull the plug."

"Ma."

"Shit." She pouts. "Can't count on you guys for nothing. Guess I'm gonna have to get that tattoo. DO NOT RESUSCITATE!" She scrawls it across her chest with her gear-shifting hand. "Al. You make a bookmark from my hair. Make a bunch, and keep me in all your favorites." She pats Bob's leg. "Make yourself the best paintbrush, Bobby. Paint me something beautiful!" She slaps and pinches his cheeks without looking from the road.

"Prolly did it running over trash," the man from AAA says. "A box or a sign or loose metal." He smiles, shaking his head. He tightens the tow chains to the car. "See it all the time. You folks from around here?" Ma ignores the small talk. "Too late to get it fixed; you want me to drop you off at a hotel?"

Ma says, "Yes, that would be great," and nothing else. The rest of the ride to Albert Lea, the four of us sit shoulder-to-shoulder in the silent truck.

Being around Ma doesn't let me pretend to be someone else, so while she talks to the kid at the front desk, leaning on the counter like it's holding her up, I call Lindy and ask her to come get Julie and me. I whisper to Julie that we're going to leave.

Ma walks toward us, smiling and flashing the key card.

"We're going to take off," I say. "Lindy is going to come get us. She'll be here in an hour or so."

"What? Um . . . OK," she says, confused and weary. "Whatever you want to do, Al." She sits next to Julie on the couch. "Is she coming right now? I'll wait with you guys."

"You don't have to, Ma."

She gives me a look.

The teenager behind the desk taps into his computer while we wait. Julie and I grope each other like no one's around and Ma's face hardens and turns red. She walks off and looks out the motel's glass doors, then looks in a potted plant and picks at the dirt.

Lindy's minivan arrives, and Ma picks up a suitcase and shuffles outside.

"Later, Ma," I say, avoiding her eyes, pecking her cheek.

"Love you so much, Ali." She swats the side of my face and then hugs Julie. "Have fun, you guys. Call me."

IV

1997–1999

I'M SWALLOWING MYSELF ALIVE. HAPPY'S HALLOWED EVE brumbles into Weeks of Pleasing Myself. I celebrate the ticking seconds of every goddamn day. I'm a festival, a parade, and the drinks are vicious. There is cake and blood-slick flesh.

These are the Nights of Atoning for Nothing. Star-Pied Afternoons.

I blink and I'm outside the party at the Crack House, ghosting from the backyard into Saint Paul's night, scratching my neck's mosquito bites until they bleed. I wake in a pile of trash bags, hands sticky and red. In front of me on the sidewalk, a spilled coffee can, cigarette butts like tiny dead mice. It's junglewalk humid, and I'm sopping wet. I shotgun the beer I find in my pocket.

After shaking the can, I launch the beer into the clouds above Grand Avenue, and it's pierced by a star. The darkness stills, and as we tip back to watch, moonbright climbs down our bodies. I smile at each of the watershed faces, slashes in the whispering trees. It's almost morning, midnight, and noon.

When I blink up, the can is still hovering in the clouds. I'm on campus again, friends sleeking through the shadows. The can hangs and there's time to drink one more. To harass the shifty-eyed pizza deliveryman, grab Julie and pry into kiss. Tongue in her mouth as the beer explodes down.

And each time my girlfriend takes me back to her room, each time I lead another girl away, I might as well be watching the fucking on TV. I sit on the other side of the room while bodies divide from clothes. Flooded skin and held limbs, hands over a mouth, a roommate *ooops*es the door closed. Boss and black and blue and skin sinking in the wet spot. Again and again—the unpurest of bones and flesh rock 'n' rolling together.

It's feverish, this not-feeling-anything. This Feast of Forgetting to Be Afraid.

V

March 1998

MY MOUTH IS RED-CAPED AND JAGGED WHEN I SNAP THE chain and the bulb shudders to life. I towel the blood away, and a scarlet line paints from my right nostril, over my lips, and down the left side of my chin. Blood drips, lushes over the sink. My heart juggles like a bone in my throat.

Casey bursts through the door, looking around like he's being chased. His ashen face is mud-streaked and grinning. He's got no idea that this is our room, that I'm his roomie. Blinking, tapping his stomach, he drags himself to the couch.

"Ey, man. Yo, Case, you OK? You fucked up?" I throw blood-soaked tissues at him and then make sure none of my teeth are gone or chipped.

He turns mechanically, says, "You should have come

with," and then tells me about getting fucked up and sprinting through the woods along the banks of the Mississippi. He walks to the window and lights up.

"Yeah?" I snort through my nosebleed.

"Oh shit. Al." He gapes at me like, *poof,* I just Houdinied into the room. "You're bleeding! Damn." He says it again, louder—"Damn!"—and I drool blood onto the hardwood floor.

Casey flinches big-eyed and scooches back when I stick out my tongue.

"You should do something about your ugly fucking face." He asks how the baseball party was.

With toilet paper pressed to my mouth, I point at the Marlboro cigarette sign I tore off of Park Liquor. A flimsy piece of ripped and blood-smeared Styrofoam board. "Piece-of-shit party." I wince and smile. "Face-planted. Can you tell? One minute, I'm sprinting down Snelling carrying that shitty-ass sign, and then BOOM! Right on my fuckin' face."

Blood curtains my teeth and I spit and tell him about the strippers, running home after the party, how Keenan jogged with his video camera focused ahead at the street. Between drags, Casey mashes his forehead against the window like he wants to swan-dive from the second story.

The sink fills with dozens of Rorschach tests as we talk.

"Thank God that shit was deserted, Case. I'd be tits up."

"Seriously. That shit is nasty." He points a dirty finger at me and smiles. "You need stitches. A tampon or something."

When it finally stops bleeding, I open another beer and sit on the radiator. Morning birds coo outside.

"Al. Yo. Al. You gotta boogie if you want to catch that bus. Get a move on, man. I'll see you next week." Casey drops the smoke in a soda can, slaps me five, and hops in bed. "Don't forget your mitt, jackass. And hit the light when you bounce."

WHEN I'M FACE-SLAPPED AWAKE, EVERYTHING IS QUAKING—I have no idea where I am. Rows of seats. The backs of heads. An intercom voice. With the room swooping from side to side, I try to stand, but I'm winched down. Gasping, I squeeze the safety belt and rub my eyes. Dripping with sweat, I look out the window just as the airplane squawks down. A stewardess welcomes us to Fort Myers.

"Hey, Al. Spring break, brah," Keenan laughs. "You in there?"

When I grin it feels like someone stabbed me in the mouth.

The team deplanes down the aisles, single file in our blue tracksuits like a chain gang. A sunburned family wanders by us in the airport. Riding down the escalator to the luggage carousel, we watch a group of girls strip off their winter clothes.

"What happened to your face?" Matt asks as the team vans pull up. Keenan laughs and tells him the story as we load up the bat and helmet bags.

"You stupid fucker, Happy." Matt shakes his head.
Kevin says he should see the video of me dancing
around, trying to talk after I fell.

"Fucking classic," Kevin howls.

I give them a little bow and slide the door open for
them.

WE TAKE INFIELD BEFORE THE FIRST GAME, AND I TRY TO SOAK
all of it in. Coach hits grounders to the second base-
man and the shortstop with the fungo—the infielders
scoop the snake rapers up and then smoothly wing the
ball to first, where it pops into Kevin's mitt. For a
while, I forget everything that's wrong with me. I can't
believe I'm playing again. I don't care that I'm in right
field.

The sky is oceanic. The grass looks like glass. My
heart thunders like it's trying to push out of me.

When it's not my turn to catch a practice fly ball, I
watch two kids chase each other across the street.
One reaches into the weeds and then hurls a rock
at the other boy. A car stereo—playing Biggie Smalls's
"Hypnotize"—shudders the air. Bugs fly loops around
me.

Justin, our catcher, throws the last warm-up pitch
down to second on a clothesline. The ump gruffs "Play
ball!" and the dugouts chatter. Coach is all business
behind his Oakley sunglasses, signaling pitches to Justin as the first batter steps into the box. Kurt takes the
sign and fans stand, clapping and shouting. Dad and

Lindy are somewhere up there. It smells like hot dogs and sunscreen and my rank skin.

Staring around the baseball diamond, I keep imagining Ma and Bob leaning into the left-field fence. Back in Iowa Falls, instead of lawn furniture they'd bring straight-backed wooden chairs—the ones from our dinner table—and sit in the shadows. Glass plates steamed in their laps. "You have to have real food," Ma would say when I ran out between innings. "You want some, Tiny?" Hustling back to the dugout, I could hear her yelling, "It's real food!" and smacking her lips.

Catching behind the plate, three hundred feet away from them, I could smell the roasted chicken and rice and sweet potatoes and beets. Their scrunched wads of tinfoil shone in the fence. Pennants of smoke swirled into the outfield when Bob smoked his after-dinner cigar.

My teammates would laugh, asking if I could hear the crazy shit Ma was yelling. "Good eye," she'd shout when one of our batters took a ball. "Good eye!" Then "Hey, batter" or "Swing, batta, swing!" without a player standing in the box. Even "We want a pitcher" or "Push 'em back, push 'em back, waaaaay back." She didn't care if she mixed up her sports; she loved it. When I was up to bat, I'd step out of the box, look past Coach Collison's signals at third, and see her rattling the outfield fence. "Good eyes! Good teeth!" Ma'd yell. "You bet! Good ears! You gotta have 'em! Good bones! Good bones! Good bones! Go Iowa Falls!" Chanting like a protestor, she'd lift the enormous cardboard circle she'd painted into a GO I.F. baseball high above the fence.

The neurologists cleared me to play if I would play outfield, but I don't know what I'm doing. I've been a catcher since fourth grade; I've never played another position. I pose how I think a right fielder should and look to see if anyone's watching. I pull at my nut cup, bury a cleat, and tear up a yard of dirt. I blow spit bubbles and cluck my tongue, then go back to swatting the clouding insects.

When the aluminum bat pings, I'm watching the palm fronds. I look at the plate but the batter is running to first. My teammates yell, pointing into the air, but I can't move. Keenan sprints toward me from second, searching over his shoulder, an arm arrowing into the sky. I stare right into the sun.

The ballpark flurries around me, and then the moment stretches. All of the diamond's sounds flatten into one tone, and then, *pop*, there's a sharp nothing. I screen my eyes with my glove and look again but only see orange haloes. A hundred jumping suns. I start running, but out of the corner of my eye, I see the baseball drop into the grass.

Time begins racing when I throw the ball to third. Sunshine drills down and the air tightens. The runner is on second, clapping. Kurt walks back to the mound, kicking the grass and yelling, "Bullshit!" I pull my hat down and jog toward the fence.

"Shake it off, Al," Keenan yells behind me.

The Impala is stopped in the road. The two boys are

sitting on the curb, shading their eyes and watching. I can hear Coach shout above the burbling crowd. Someone's booing.

"Get better," Coach screams at me. "Get better! You need to get better!"

"Fuck you all." I turn and spit toward my teammates in the dugout, then cover my grin with my glove. *You fucks have no idea.* It feels so good to be playing again. This shit is glorious.

"Better than last year, isn't it, Al?" My father laughs loudly, springing silverware from the table when he drops his arms. "Sure is, huh? Isn't this great?" He smiles and grips my shoulder.

The restaurant is a hatchery of candlelight. Dinnerware clinks. At other tables, couples converse in whispers. I combed and spiked my hair and threw on a sleazebag-looking Hawaiian shirt for dinner. Lindy said, "Very nice," and straightened my collar, but sunburned, my face cut up, I must look insane.

She tells me how proud they are of me.

"You better believe it," Dad says, taking a bite of his filet. Lindy puts her hand over mine as he speaks. "You've worked your tail off to get back here." But what I hear makes it seem like they're talking about someone else.

"No kidding." Each time I speak my face feels like it's splitting open. My chest tightens. "It's nice to be here."

Dad asks if I got my ass kicked again and laughs, says I'm lucky to have such a hard head. "Like me," he says, guffawing and sipping beer. "A lemonhead."

When I get back to the Del Prado Inn, my teammates are jostling around the pool, laughing and watching Django dance. He races around in a tiny wrestling singlet, huffing his bottom lip and yapping. The spandex is Corvette red with an oversized, block-letter USA on the chest. Django chases the guys with outstretched arms, asking for hugs. After sprinting around the pool a few times, he jogs up the diving board steps and springs from the wobbling fiberglass. In the air, he tucks into a V and then unfolds and knifes into the pool.

Hollers rise into the dark as I walk to my room for some gin and pills.

Django is prancing on a roof next to the pool when I get back. He pounds his chest like King Kong and sings incomprehensibly. The guys peg him with empty cans, yell at him to come down. A can hits him in the head and he screams and runs and jumps, floating over the water, flailing and yelling "Spring break, bitches!" as he curls. The massive cannonball makes it rain. Flipping chairs and leaping the fence, we sprint back to our rooms.

While my teammates play hearts and euchre or get ready for bed, I sneak back to the pool and sit in the dark. I listen to the DJ Kool CD I stole from Casey and pick the scab on my face. My bottom lip is raw from chewing Skoal all day, so I jam the burning tobacco between my top lip and gums.

I spit into the pool where Django landed and the phlegm pops and sags in the waves. When I'm sure no one's coming out, I scatter the chew into the pool, crumple a Coke can, and key-pop holes in it so I can smoke out of it. A frog barks in the canal behind the motel while I spark the lighter.

It's great you're even playing—each game someone says it to me. It makes me feel like I'm a gold medalist in the Special Olympics.

A long time after I smoke and the painkillers I ate have softened my bones, I lose track of the wave I've been following in the pool. I find a hunk of leftover steak in the doggy bag and rest it on my tongue. I don't chew; I want to savor the taste, see how long it takes to dissolve. My shirt is wet from the chair, but under the half-lit Florida sky, I'm back. I'm playing again. I'm fucked up and happy.

VI

1

Staring down the plummeting street, it feels like Julie and I are trapped on a roller coaster. She shrieks when I squeeze her thigh and we laugh and kiss. I wrench back the parking brake and look out at the hillside mansions. They're all pristine, photographs from architecture and design magazines. Climbing vines and rosebushes and ornate shrubbery. After skipping around the car, Julie grabs my hand and we walk into the plot where her family's new home is being built.

"It's going to be great, isn't it?" She kisses my cheek.

"It's going to be fucking huge." I laugh.

"We'll have something like this someday! We will!"

"Pretty amazing." The hedges look like stylists and mathematicians trimmed them. "Look at these fucking places."

"Oh, I can't wait until it's done." She dances around the landscaped lot, blueprinting their home for me. Pointing out the bedrooms. Her father's office. The living room and entertainment den. A picture window that'll have a million-dollar view of Mt. Hood.

And the horizon *is* incredible. I can see everything. Portland, Hillsboro, Beaverton, Lake Oswego. Vancouver, probably. Julie points at her parents' house, where we're living this summer, and then turns the opposite way and points toward the gym I work at.

"It's going to be perfect!"

The sun reflects off of the mountains' snowy peaks and I know that this—my relationship with Julie—is over. I half listen and try to smile, fighting off the urge to tell her that I'm going to leave her soon. That I'm going to go back to Iowa for the rest of the summer because I'm cheating on her again.

JULIE SHOULD HAVE BROKEN UP WITH ME LAST SUMMER when I visited her in Portland. When I told her that I'd cheated on her she paled, then started crying. I mumbled and lied, said it had only been once, that I'd been wasted, blacked out. After pushing me away, she ran upstairs and a door slammed. I walked into the kitchen and slipped a butcher knife from the wooden block. Gripping it in front of my chest, I listened to her muffled weeping and then slammed the blade into my left wrist. When the skin started to petal open I was overcome with shame—the perpendicular cut was on the top of my forearm. I couldn't even do this right. Julie came back an hour later, eyes pearly and red. I was watching the news with bloody paper towels in my lap. Julie stood above me, mouth agape, and asked what had happened. Instead of telling her that it had nothing to do with her, that I was confused about everything and couldn't feel anything anyway, I shrugged. I said I didn't know what I was doing and then started to cry.

2

THE DAY I LEAVE JULIE, THE SUN DROPS OUTSIDE OF SPOKANE like the entire West Coast is on fire. Far past midnight I flick the headlights on and off and sing as much of the alphabet as I can before fear makes me slash them back on. I jerk the steering wheel to get the Oldsmobile between the lines. I'm twitchy with drugs, but I sing more letters each time, and they roll into the dark— my heart big-swinging in my chest—until I am breathless. Under the moonlight, the fields look ice-glazed and I drive with the headlights off, waiting for something to happen. But the headlights stay off. Windows down, I feel fleshless. The stars are a spray of needleholes in the sky.

3

Halloween 1998

"Spanked it into a sock," I laugh, "going a hundred miles per hour. I had to move, man, move!" Lars looks like a blowfish, bulge-eyed and cheeks popping, while I talk about breaking up with Julie in Portland. How I masturbated into a tube sock as my Oldsmobile sped through Idaho, fifteen hours after leaving her. Casey says, "Classy," and jerks his hand up and down. Hamm's beer squirts from Lars's pinched lips.

"Twenty-five straight hours of driving, man. I was all fucked up when I got to Mason City. Listened to that Geto Boys song 'bout a million times. Must have looked like roadkill when I walked in. Pops didn't know what the fuck to think."

Casey raps, *"I make big money, I drive big cars, everybody know me, it's like I'm a movie star!"* as a pack of girls in St. Olaf jerseys and running panties sprints by. Legs bare. A few have mittens on. The pre-race thrum of the cross-country meet fills Como Park.

"You should have crashed with me," Lars smacks. Bits of chewing tobacco dot his lips like fruit flies. "Blue Earth, baby!"

"I needed to get home. Only stopped for smoke, caffeine, and gas. It felt like—"

"Baaah!" Casey shouts. "Blue Earth is doo-doo. Should have come up to the Cities for whippits. The funky monkey and me and whippits!" He points down the hill where Yarrow, my new girlfriend, is running with her teammates. Her short ponytail swings with her strides. Lars drops his beer and windmills after them until he falls down and lies flat.

"You chumps aren't going to make it out tonight," Casey says when Lars gets back. "You'll be out cold before we put our costumes on."

"Bullshit." Lars laughs breathlessly. Fall leaves flutter around us on the golf course, crimson and orange and carmine.

While we stumble to the starting line I tell them about working at Gold's Gym while I lived with Julie in Oregon. How I spent my days flirting with women who shouldn't have been wearing spandex. *That's it, just like that.* I smiled, helping their makeup-mopped faces get one more rep. *Great work! Fantastic!* The other trainers and I wore the carpet down around the thong-wearing hotties, flashing the trophy wives that *yeah-you-know-what-I-like* look. We salivated at them through the office's closed blinds like stalkers. "Lifting weights and eating tuna," I crow. "I was king of the fucking world!"

"Nice work, Lemon," Casey says. "Indeed, hombre."

Yarrow and Liz and MK streak by again, a blur of blue and orange and skin, calves flexing with each step. We shout, "Way to go, Mac!" but the girls don't look.

"Oh yeah, and I met this girl at the gym," I smile. "Older. Trouble, you know?" I pretend shock. "She took advantage of me!"

Lars squints and lifts his cigarette and inhales. "Yeah?" He tinks his beer against mine and laughs, "HELL YEAH!" He pushes at Casey's smoke but Casey punches his hand away. "What happened? Why don't you ever talk about her, Motlow?" Lars yells because the PA voice starts getting shrill. "You don't say shit, man!"

"We gotta go," I say, ignoring him. "Time to do this." I still haven't figured out why the fuck he calls me "Motlow"—it's just another line on my list of nicknames.

"Fucking Captain Mysterio, here," Casey says, flicking the cigarette at me. "Marty told me you don't go to class. Just walk around getting fucked up, huh?"

"Nope. Wasn't me." I laugh. "Wait. Do I get a cape?"

"Fuck it. Let's just sit here," Lars sighs.

"You suck, Lemon."

"I love you guys!" I laugh.

We toss the beers into the weeds and then stumble

down the slope to the start. Each tottering step I take flakes more porcelain clay from my art studio jeans. When the gun goes off, the crowd explodes into cheers.

JULIE'S PARENTS HAD WELCOMED ME INTO THEIR HOME THIS summer—I lived in an extra bedroom. Money, job, food, they helped with everything I might possibly need. Driving to work, I drank, got fucked up on pills or whatever I had. It was lavish.

I'd been working at Gold's Gym for a few weeks when Kate and I ended up making out in the laundry room. That night we were in the backseat of a 4Runner when I called Julie to say I'd be home late. A week and a half later, I packed my bags and lied, told Julie that I was going back to Iowa because she was suffocating me. I lived with a friend for two more weeks so I could see Kate every day and party with her every night.

I went back at summer's end and Kate and I spent a weekend on the Oregon coast. "Beautiful day at the beach," she said, biting my ear, her hand burrowing into my jeans as we lay in the cold sand. Gray waves crashed, pulled back as we kissed.

But after returning to Minnesota, I couldn't remember what she looked like. "I think I'm pregnant," the voice on the phone said the third week of the semester. I held it away from my ear and with my other hand typed an e-mail to Yarrow. The voice wanted to know what we were going to do, how we could make our relationship work, while I asked Yarrow when we could get together again. I sighed with concern and *hmmmm*ed into the phone. Each keystroke crunched because a few weeks earlier, someone had unloaded a fire extinguisher through a slit cut in our screen window. The yellow dust was everywhere, corroding our electronics.

I avoided Kate the next weeks. Casey would say that she called and smile, ask who Kate was. "Don't know," I'd say, closing my bedroom door as he laughed. I'd tear his Post-its off my computer and drop them in the trash. Pretend like her e-mails weren't clogging up my in-box.

When we finally talked last week, Kate told me she'd gone to Planned Parenthood. There was no baby after all, she sighed. "That's good," was about all I said. The line got quiet and I coughed. "Yeah, that's really great."

THE SHEETS ARE DRY WHEN I ROLL, KNUCKLING MY GROIN TO see if I pissed the bed again. I quietly rifle bags and drawers, sniffing my bedroom for vomit, laughing, "Motherfucker," because this has become a morning ritual. I'm bound to throw up a blood-flecked mess later, so I decide to go gag myself in the shower, but my guts seize when I open the door. Yarrow is splayed out on the couch in her cheerleader costume, red and blue ribbons tousling her hair. She looks dead.

Frozen in the doorway, at first, I'm stunned and

heartbroken. She's unmoving: a leg ratcheted to the floor, miniskirt flipped up. And then I get mad. A minute passes, and I go from stunned to tired. And then, staring into my dingy living room, I'm just curious. A half-eaten sandwich and two oranges sit atop the fridge. The bluegray dimness reeks of minnows. Within five minutes, I come to grips with having done something terrible last night, and after wincing at Yarrow's still shape, I shoulder it all off and don't feel much of anything. As I hunch over her—wondering what the fuck I did—Yarrow exhales and scratches her cheek.

"Why didn't you sleep with me?" I ask angrily, shaking the sleep from her. "Huh?"

She blinks, her face stiffening as she takes in the room. "You wouldn't let me, that's why." She stands, sloughs me off. "You weren't making any sense, Al, just kept pushing me out of bed. What the hell?"

I remember smoking a joint with a caveman and the Incredible Hulk by the door to the party. A closed-room drug-huddle. Dan was standing in the kitchen in his Speedo with Snow White. The Toxic Avenger. A witch. Casey and Kirkman were laughing in the front yard when I stumbled out. Dangling to the waist of their velvet tracksuits, spray-painted chains smoldered gold in the light.

"Yeah, sure," Yarrow says after I apologize. "Whatever." The door slams. I lean out of the window as she passes, tell her that I'll call in a bit, but she doesn't stop walking.

Happy

The shower water slaps my back while I empty myself. On my hands and knees, gagging and heaving, I realize that I'm always afraid, waiting to do something dreadful. It's inevitable. I puke and black grains and blood whorl in the drain.

I lie on the floor when I get back from the bathroom. The message light on the phone winks in front of me. The first one is from Ma—"Boo!" she yells. The second one is from Ma, too. "Happy happy Halloweeeeeeeeeen!" she sings. Lars is the third—"Motlow, Motlow, Motlow! Where the fuck you go, man? Yeah, so, let's see here . . . I think Abe Lincoln just grabbed my package. What do you think? Should I give it to him?"

The empty booze bottles that had lined the bookshelf are on the floor. They're all cracked. It looks like someone stomped on them.

Ma shook her head when she saw my bottle collection the last time she visited. "What are those?" she asked disgustedly. "Pretty stupid stuff, Al. Hope you're taking care of yourself."

"Ma, it's fine. They're fine. Don't worry about it."

"You should take them down." She frowned. "What are they even for?"

"Ma, will you quit buggin' me?" I scowled at her. "I don't know why Casey is keeping them!"

"That's some stupid shit if you ask me. You tell him."

4

November

WHEN CASEY AND I SHOVE INTO THE PARTY "GHETTO SUPER-
star" is playing so loudly it feels like I'm being punched
in the chest. Mashing bodies sing and dance in the
soggy air. Birdcalls and bodysweat. The thudding walls
smell like melting gumballs and kerosene. In the front
hall, Julie and Erin are lying in a pile of coats, laughing
and sharing an enormous plastic cup, lips violet in the
wrung-out light. Plaster bits rain through the jerky
brightness.

I hold my arms out going down the stairwell to the
basement, tracing my fingers through the condensation. X-mas lights are braided through the pipes in the
ceiling. In the corner, a jam band looks like they're
sweating Kool-Aid.

I point at a couch and Casey shakes his head. He

shouts, "Later!" and slides into the jungle of people, heading for the keg.

For hours, the party cords around the basement while I fingernail labels off of the four beers I brought. I'm taking a night off—Casey caught me throwing up in my bedroom yesterday, and a couple of weeks ago, a bunch of funny fuckers started calling me Alkie. That same week Yarrow said that when she first transferred to Mac, someone told her that they thought I was gay because I was so different than most jocks. I laughed it off to each of them, but all of it's been gnawing me apart.

"Hey, Case. How you doing, man?" I ask when he crawls out of the partying tide and sits. The bottles' slimy confetti covers my jeans.

"Good, Al." He rubs his hands together, milks his thumbs. "Things are shaping up." He grins. "How 'bout you? You doing OK?"

"Chilling. Taking it easy." I point to the dancing mass. "Jumaane was looking for you. Seth, too. He's somewhere around this fucking place."

We sit on the moldy couch, deafened and nodding at the friends who pass. Everyone boos when the lights come on. Austin squeezes between us and points up like he's talking about God, then whispers, "Let's go," and smiles crazily. He stands and pushes his way up the clogged stairs. The lights go out again, and everyone claps and screams.

"Hey, Golden," Lens says when we walk in. "What's the haps, Happy?" The bedroom is ferned and quivering with smoke. Austin is lying in a bed, wild eyed and grinning. Seth asks us what's going on.

"Nada," I say glumly. "Not even a little bit o' shit."

Casey tells him to suck it, then laughs and slaps him five and we sardine into the circle of people.

The room fills with coughing and jokes and laughter, and then it's all a constant purr, my friends putting themselves away in the blistery, getting-fucked-up air. For an hour, I pass each time the bong is handed to me. "Nope," I laugh. "Tonight, my body is a temple!" I say no thanks to the drinks and shrooms and blow.

During an aimless story, I bail, pissed and bored, and rummage through the bathroom's cabinets and drawers. Below, the stereo in the living room shuts off. There's a laugh, diluted talking. Outside in the street, breaking glass and shouting.

The blue smog is velvety when I open the door again. Everyone looks up with bloodshot eyes, pauses for a second, and then busts out laughing. By the time I sit, all of the mouths are singing, muttering again.

"Can't believe that shit happened," Casey says, gripping the bong like a saxophone. Blue smoke trellises along the walls.

I smile, waiting for the punch line to Casey's joke. Ready to call him a fuck or a douche bag.

"Blood in his brain, man. You believe that shit?" He conjures through the smoke. "I mean, shit, he could've died or something."

My heart stutter-stops.

"Huh? What's that?"

"What did you say, Casey?"

"What the fuck are you talking about, Golden?" Katie giggles and throws a paper wad at him, then dismissively says, "Sure, Casey. Whatever."

"Yeah, so anyway." Lars waves Casey off and gets back to his story. "I was like, 'Rodmo, get outta my fuckin' room!'" Everyone laughs when Lars finishes, but I'm still staring at Casey.

"Al," he says. "Al." He nods his head toward me. The room tilts. "Blood in his brain, man. I took 'im to the fuckin' hospital."

"Who the fuck is Al?" Katie is annoyed. "Shit, Casey."

"What the fuck are you talking about, Golden? Fucking tool."

Kara hikes her jeans up and moves to the desktop stereo. "Requests, anyone? Don't mind Golden, he's fucking rocked."

"Oh shit!" Lens laughs hysterically. "Casey is all fucked up. Oh, shit!"

The room *oooooh*s and hollers. A Bob Marley song strings through the haze.

"You silly fucks." Casey points at me. "*That's Al.*"

Everyone looks perplexed for a second and then laughs like they aren't in on the joke. I can feel the blood draining from me.

"Man, that's *Happy*. Golden, what the fuck are you talking about? What the fuck is he talking about, *Happy?*"

I look at the bong I've just been handed and worry

my face. I shrug, mumble, "Got no fucking clue," and then smoke, opening my eyes hugely when I inhale. "He's a fucking moron," I exhale.

DAYLIGHT EVISCERATES ME. I'M IN MY BED WITH LAUREL, the sad-smiling girl I'd been talking with at Keenan's after-party. Wearing my shirt, she laughs softly when she sees me look around. I'm sure she's been waiting for me to wake up for hours; she's been sober for years.

Yesterday, Yarrow called from the cross-country meet they're at for the weekend. She said she loved me, then laughed and wondered how it slipped out. We made dinner plans for Monday and I wished her luck.

But last night is splintered, a handful of oil.

The window is webbed with frost, frigid against my forehead. Snow sweeps through the trees. Lying on top of me, looking outside, Laurel smells like cigarettes and sweetmint and sweat.

"This was bound to happen, Lo, wasn't it?"

"Yes." She slides out of bed, takes my shirt off, and kisses me. "Yes it was."

"Well, good then," I cheer. "What wonderful news!"

Our underwear and socks and jeans and jackets hang like moss from the furniture. It looks like we barely made it into my bedroom.

Laurel is cripplingly beautiful, and I've always wanted her. But half-sober in the morning light, I realize how much she intimidates me. Just watching her walk, you can tell she's got her shit together.

Her shoulder blades ridge from her tan skin when she puts her Celtic green shirt on. She finds her panties and then jumps into her jeans. "See you later?" She cocoons into her coat.

"Course." I kiss her again. I want to ask her to stay but I know I'm going to throw up soon. "See you later today, Lo." I mumble. "For sure."

We pull apart and she smiles.

"Hey, Lo? . . . Yarrow's friends live all over here, so watch out, OK?"

I sniff a can I find on the floor, gargle the flat beer, and then spit it into the trash. I unplug the phone.

The room glitters like a busted-up mirror ball as the winter afternoon darkens: our dorm is filthy with curios. I've been sticking debris on the walls with white athletic tape—attaching jeans and silverware, orange rinds and moldy pizza, paintbrushes and pots, bowls and drawings and photos, pens, beer bottles, knots of twine, T-shirts and toys, scissors, a jar of hair, matches, a lighter, and a microcassette recorder. We live in one of Joseph Cornell's castoffs, a museum of space junk.

"HELLUVA NIGHT, HUH, AL?" CASEY SHOUTS WHEN HE RUNS in. "All fish guts and gravy, right?" Laughing, he sits on the couch. "Al, what the fuck are you doing?"

"Working out." I curl a dumbbell. "You should try it. I feel like I'm gonna die. I gotta sweat some." I curl the other weight up and then press them above me.

155

"Stupid ass." He flips the TV on and tells me to move. "In the way, Al! Can't see shit!"

"Where'd you sleep?" The dumbbells clatter when I drop them. I kick-roll one of the weights to him.

"Not here," he laughs. "You hook up?"

"Shit," I mutter. "I suppose I did."

Casey smiles and mutes the TV. "Hmm, let me guess . . . Laurel?"

"Maybe. Maybe not."

"Ha! You fucker. I knew it. Yarrow's not going to like that shit." He squeals, "Oh boy! Let the good times roll!"

"Hey, Case, that girl didn't know my name, huh?" I drop to the floor and start doing sit-ups.

"Which?" Casey thwacks the remote until it works, then aimlessly flips channels.

"Girl at the party. Katie."

"Oh . . . nope. No fucking clue." *The Simpsons* is on TV; he laughs. "Pretty hilarious, that stupid bitch. *That's Happy.*" Mimicking her again—"*That's Happy*"—he jumps up and throws the couch pillows around. "You seen my light?"

"That shit happens all the time, Case"—I stand, start digging through the cushions—"and I'm just starting to notice it. Fuckin' fuckers don't know who I am. Just Happy. That's some bullshit, huh? Fucking Happy."

"Yeah, some of these assholes don't know your real name." He grins big and holds the lighter up like it's a hundred-dollar bill. "That's some funny shit, though, right? Hey, I'm going to dinner, you wanna come?"

"Nah."

"You want me to bring you something?"

"I'm cool, Case, thanks. Hey—Katie's dumb, right?" I blow smoke through the screen. Icy rain tinkles against the window frame and the heat hisses on. A scarf of smoke drifts back inside and hovers in front of the TV.

"Fuck yeah, man, already told you. A silly bitch, for sure. All those fucks that don't know your name." He watches the sleet and laughs. "Fuckin' can't wait for it to snow a ton. We'll make some forts and shit, get blazed, and sit out there all night. Let's go snowboarding."

"For sure, Case."

"Positive you don't want to come?" He opens the door to go. "You might see Laurel!" he whoops. "You're a no-good bird, Dirty Lemon!"

"No."

"Come on, man, come with. Let's go to the radio station. It's gonna be fun! Tuna fish, sucka!"

"Blah blah blah," I say, grabbing the gin. "I got work to do."

VII

1

May 1999

WHEN I RIDE UP TO THE DORM WINDOW, MY FRIENDS WILL say I look so happy I probably shit my pants, the new Trek gleaming beneath me like Hephaestus forged it from sun rays. Smiling, I laugh and turn in widening circles through the parking lot of County Cycles, hard-pedaling but going nowhere in the highest gear. The pavement looks inlaid with mirrors because of the fresh rainwater. I'm euphoric. The shifting chain, the sprockets and knobby treads whirring. The bike is perfect. I've never spent this much on anything.

It downpoured the hour I was in the bike shop but the clouds began pulling apart as I jangled outside. The salesman asked again, and I told him a second time that I didn't want a helmet. He helped me adjust the seat and tighten the brakes, then thanked me again and went back in. The gray ceiling swooshed away, brightening the sky to a blinding, immaculate blue.

I breeze through Roseville, flipping through the gears just to feel their flick and roll. My legs barely pump and the bike races down Lexington. I might beat Lars back to campus. I might ride out of my skin.

Coasting through Larpenteur Avenue, my face starts to prickle, and then the tingling drops into my neck and clavicle and chest and hands and fingertips. My eyes start to skip like frying eggs. And then, I can't feel the bike beneath me. I can't feel anything at all. The numbness courses through me and I know, instantly, that my brain is bleeding again.

The concrete rushes up and I veer, slam into a curb. I fly headfirst over the handlebars and face-skid in the grass. I roll and the bike lands on top of me.

Five minutes later, when I realize I can move all my limbs, I throw the bike off of me and sit up. I look at the blank-windowed homes around me. The street is silent except for the gurgling gutters. My eyes are bouncing worse than they ever have and my face is numb, like someone hit me with a two-by-four. I stretch on the lawn and then get on the bike. A gray-haired man walks out of the house across the street and watches me try to regain my balance. A station wagon passes. Another car shoots through the puddles as I start to pedal, wobbly-slow, into Como Park.

Ignoring the street signs, oblivious to my wrong turns, I ride toward campus and decide not to tell anyone what just happened. If no one knows, then my brain isn't bleeding. If I don't speak about it, then there's nothing wrong with me. I'll wake tomorrow and everything will be fine. I Chinese-dragon down the middle of the road. A car honks from behind me and I grind into the curb and almost fall again. The engine whines by my pasty face.

2

AFTER THE BOX OF CERAMICS IS SNUGGLED INTO THE BACK OF the Escort, Ma jumps up on the curb, arms raised like a gymnast's. "Ta-da! Let's go, Al. Let's go!" she yells. "Faster, Ali!"

"I'm going, Ma," I say. "Shit, man. Going fast as I can."

Each time I move, I grasp at the air in front of me because I'm afraid I'm falling. Since I crashed my bike two weeks ago, I've been rigid and tired. I didn't help Casey move to his new apartment and halfheartedly said good-bye to Yarrow when she left for Thailand. I've just sat in my dark room, listening to everyone go.

"Ready to bust a move, Ali?" Ma asks, clapping and hip-rolling like she's working a hula hoop.

"One more. That's it. All she wrote."

"All right! Let's go then!" She smiles and slaps my cheeks, excited that I'm coming to live with her and Bob this summer. The pottery clinks as it settles in the car.

"Ali Baba! You ready?" she asks after I set the last box down. "This it?"

I nod, watching three guys throw a Frisbee on Shaw Field.

"Wanna get some treats? I scream, you scream, yeah yeah for ice cream!"

"Naw, I don't think so . . . Hey, Ma?"

"Yeah, Ali?"

"I haven't been feeling so good." My chest caves when I speak.

"Oh no, Al, what's up? You got the flu?" She slams the hatchback and smiles at me. "Summer colds suuuuuccckkk, dude!"

"Yep . . . But, Ma, I've been kinda dizzy." If I don't look away from her I'm going to cry. "For a while, I think. That numb thing again. My balance and stuff."

"What's going on, honey?" Her face is lily white when I look back at her. She leans on the car.

"I'm pretty sure it's my brain," I say. Staring over her at the nearly deserted campus, I tell her what's going on. "I know that's what it is, Ma. I can feel it."

She looks confused and then angry for a second. "Why did you wait so long to tell me? Shit, Ali, what the fuck are you doing? We have to see the doctor. Now!"

"Ma!" I start to weep. She pulls me down to her shoulder and tugs my hair while I bawl. "Ma. No one thought it'd happen again!"

"Oh, Ali," she says, tears glossing her face. "Oh, my baby."

3

June

Four hours ago, I walked out of the neurosurgery clinic at the U of Minnesota and the flocking med students sounded disembodied. I shuffled with my head down, slammed the door on all of the light and noise, hit the gas, and set the cruise at eighty. The Twin Cities shrunk to nothing in the rearview, and the cloudless day became one big blue ecstasy. My truck is colder than a meat locker.

Since I told Ma what happened, it's been a month of MRIs and tests. Doctors held the new films to the light, pinched their chins and pointed, and then told me what I'd already known, what I'd already felt inside me—the malformation had started bleeding again. For weeks, I've been ping-ponging between neurosurgeon appointments and talking to Ma on the phone about my options. Nothing seems real anymore—I feel like I've been shot into space.

Just outside of Ames, Iowa, I lock up the brakes and skid the truck to a stop on the roadside. I'm not even halfway back to Ma's house in Oklahoma. Cornfields curlicue green to the westward horizon. Draped in sunlight, the leafy stalks bend together and then apart like a verdant ocean of sign language.

I kill the engine, turn on the hazards, and then head-butt the steering wheel. Boiling glue pours through me—I'm hot and then numb and sick. It's happening again. Fuck me, it keeps happening. My brain is bleeding. It won't stop bleeding.

I throw the cell phone off of the dashboard and then flop over the seat and curl up in the back of the cab. The truck frame rocks as cars whoosh by. I feel like a pint glass, slowly filling, brimming over, bubbling with blood.

MA'S READING LAMP IS ON IN THE LIVING ROOM WHEN I PULL into the driveway. It's the middle of the night and as I watch through the porch window, I can hear her half-asleep breathing.

"I want to do the surgery," I say instead of kissing her hello or telling her what happened. Her face puddings. "Ma, I've made up my mind."

4

July

MORTGAGE LIFTER. PORTER. RADIATOR CHARLIE. THERE
are so many tomatoes in the garden behind Ma and
Bob's house that it's impossible to remember which
fruit is which. I kneel on the wooden planks, finger-
ing the leaves, eyeing tomatoes for the salad Ma told
me to make for dinner. Each time I think I've
decided on one, palming it, ready to pluck, I second-
guess myself.

It's been like this all summer. I'm frazzled and para-
lyzed, afraid I'll fuck up. I'm afraid anything I hold
will turn to shit. All day, I sit in my bed listening to the
washing machine's two indolent notes—*thum-bump*—
or ride my bike on the iron-red roads.

"What are you doing, Ali?" Ma asks. She's standing
in the doorway to the garage/art studio, a picket of

sunflowers at her shoulder. "What's up with your face? You OK?"

"What?" I didn't realize I was touching it. I start twisting off tomatoes. "Sure, Ma, I'm fine."

"Well, make sure you get some good 'maters." She grabs a pitchfork and smiles. "Got to get into that mulch pile." With the sun in her eyes, it looks like she's cringing at me.

MA'S SCULPTURES ILLUMINATE THE OKLAHOMA DUSK. A DOLL wired to a metal porch column shines, one eyed, under the moon.

Now that I've decided on a brain surgeon, there's nothing to do but wait. I watch the night sky and Ma hums. A trio of pickups thunder by and gravel smoke scuds the dark. On the other side of town, bottle rockets fizz and pop in the air above the high school. Ma and I sit on the quiet steps until the bugs get so bad we have to go inside.

Dr. Nussbaum must be the youngest surgeon I've talked to, and I liked him right away. I joked with Ma about his peach fuzz after the first visit at the U of Minnesota, but he had talked about the brain stem and vascular malformations like a genius, a nervous prodigy. He was deliberate and serious, and his lisp oddly comforted me; it made him seem like a real person. Each appointment he'd been generous with his time, answering all of my questions and speaking amiably to Ma when she called and then called back again and again. But the decision was easiest because he was kind; he was the only brain surgeon who made me feel good.

Lying stomach-down in the oven-hot living room, I flip through art books and look at Ma's postcard collection. Reading in her La-Z-Boy, she takes long, sighing sips of ice water. Every half hour she pushes the electric fan away, stands and groans, then grabs the drying washcloth from my neck and shuffles to the bathroom to take a cool bath. When she comes back, her dress is soaked and dripping over the hardwood floor and she drops the damp washcloth on my neck.

"Go to bed, Bob," she says, taking her reading glasses off. He's snoring on the floor, a Cormac McCarthy novel flat open on his chest. The landscape painting he was working on today is angled against the wall. Oil paints still shiny and wet. "Bob. Go to bed. Go to bed."

"Wasn't sleeping," he mumbles, eyes closed. "Reading. Good book." He stands and yawns, says, "Nope," and then stumbles into their bedroom and closes the door.

I grin at Ma, and she frowns and shakes her head like she's upset, then smiles big. "Hey, Al, you want some ice cream? Maybe we should have a little?" Her voice rises when she says *little*, and she warms her hands together. "I think we should!"

"I'm going to take a bath." I say it disinterestedly. "I'm all cruddy from riding my bike. Need to scrub."

"Sure, Ali. Whatever you want." She exhales and

opens the book and slips her glasses back on. "It'll be in there if you want some."

"I won't . . . But thanks, Ma."

After I get into the water, I pyramid the rocks I've been collecting on the tub's edge. An aloe plant on the windowsill. Wildflower clippings and Spanish saint candles. A plastic statue of St. Francis. I slip the stones into the water and they scurry the tub bottom beneath me like fingernails on a blackboard. My knees rise from the hot water like red suns.

Last year at college, I'd look up from my computer screen and an X-acto knife would be cradled in my fingers like a toothpick. Between the gaps in my teeth, I'd have sliced my gums just enough so the bottle of chew spit on my desk would cloud red when I hacked into it.

I gouge my kneecaps with the stones and it feels good.

After the water cools a little, I drain a few inches away and then, slick with sweat, fill the tub with scalding water. Ma moves around, picking up books from the piles, writing on a clipboard. For a few minutes, the radio is on. She walks into the kitchen, scribbles a note to herself on the kitchen table, and then starts opening cupboards. Her singing gets louder and louder until she's outside the bathroom door, saying my name.

"Going to make some popcorn, Ali." She knocks softly. "Don't tell anyone! It's gonna taste sooo soooo good! You want some?"

"I'll be out in a bit, Ma." She keeps talking, but I slide beneath the water. When I come up, I hear the pot clanging on the stove. The popcorn pings against the pan she's using as a lid. The kernels machine-gun. She churns the pot on the burner and sings full throated.

It's one in the morning when I come out of the bathroom, but the living room is still sweltering, like the center of the earth. It's dark except for Ma's reading lamp. Lounging in the cone of light, she smiles at me.

"Going to bed, Ma."

"You!" She points and grins. "Love you, Ali. You really so tired? You don't want to stay up and party? We got corn and ice cream, man. It's early!"

"I need to sleep," I say, but we both know I'm lying. I'm going to lie in bed, fitfully rolling for hours like I have each night this summer. Listening to Ma and Bob snore in the next room, I will sit up and handwrite letters to the people I love. For weeks, I've been unable to pick up the phone, so I stay awake, writing down all of the things I'd tell them if I could call.

"You got no stamina!" she laughs.

"Yeah, it's pitiful, I know. Just too late for me." I reach down, hug her, and grab a handful of the popcorn she's covered in nutritional yeast. "Good stuff, Ma." I peck her cheek.

"You doing OK? Anything I can do?" She kisses me on the cheek again and holds my hand. "I love you, Ali. You let me know."

5

Mid-July

WITH RAIN SPLATTING THE WINDSHIELD LIKE CHUM, I GET into the Twin Cities hours before my appointment— Dr. Nussbaum and I are going to finalize the date for my surgery this afternoon. I'm excited and cagy and ready to get this shitstorm settled.

But the streets I've driven over hundreds of times are confusing. Pavement glistens. Strangers explode through puddles, their faces undefined and slick, like shapes moving through a steam room. I get lost driving the few miles from Macalester to Uptown and spend an hour parked in someone's driveway. The windows fog and I sweat.

At the Electric Fetus I clip through CDs, pretend to look at album covers when someone glances over. Occasionally, I hold one to my face, but I hardly know which ones I set on the counter. "Oh, man, a good one!" the clerk says, and I nod and smile and blearily hand over my credit card. In the truck, I look through the CDs, trying to figure out what he was talking about. With an iced coffee I pace the aisles of a used-book store. After forty-five minutes, I'm tapped on the shoulder, and when I look up from the floor, the man from the front register skittishly asks if I need any help. The thin books and colors of the crafts section loom around me. I say no thanks and leave.

The rain stops while I'm putting between red lights in downtown Minneapolis, looping around the Metrodome. After driving over the Washington Avenue Bridge and through part of the West Bank of the U of Minnesota, I circle around campus and park on River Road. I stare at the slurry of numbers on my cell phone and then call Ma, but no one answers. I redial and let it ring and ring.

The summer wind dries the windshield while I sit. I have fifteen minutes, so I ooze myself out and lie in the boulevard's wet grass. All of the trees along the Mississippi are buoyant, stunning the air thick and sweet. I close my eyes and listen to the joggers across the street—the shoes sound like a drummer rim-shotting a snare.

My watch beeps five minutes to go and I stand and clap. A passing med student smiles at me, and I nod, open my hand *hello*, but when I smile back, anger burns up my throat. I pocket my hands and cross the street, forcing myself not to glance back. I want to tackle her, cover her mouth, and tell her that I've been pretending that nothing is wrong with me for years. I want to wrench her hair and explain how, right now, I am two blocks from the neurosurgeon who's going to fix me.

When Dr. Nussbaum says he doesn't want to perform the surgery everything around me crumbles. The white walls spin and tumble. He won't do it. It doesn't matter who does. I know what it means—it means it's impossible. I look up from the floor as he talks, but I'm imagining myself cold, purple-lipped on an operating table, neurosurgeons swearing above my life-fleeing body.

"I want to be honest with you, Alex," he says. "I'm as capable as any brain surgeon in the Midwest, but because of the malformation's location in the brain stem, you might be better off in another surgeon's hands."

He stops explaining, looks down at me, and adjusts his glasses, then continues lisping precisely. He wants to introduce me to his mentor, a neurosurgeon who practices in Miami, one of the best in the world. The examination room is a fugue. Each bone in my body feels like it's pulling apart. It doesn't matter what I do. The rest of the appointment I see myself dying on an operating table.

Walking out of the neurology clinic, all of the lab coats and medical students—stethoscopes like nooses of light—whisk around me. They converse normally, but I can hear it underneath their tongues: they're whispering about me. I begin to sob. Snot runs over my lips as I ride the escalator up.

6

August

I RISE FROM THE FIELD I'VE BEEN SLEEPING NAKED IN, sunburned and pocked from neck to ass with grit. At
night, farmers have been burning their fields to the
ground, and around me, smoke fingers up from the
mile-long rows of charred, whiteblack dirt.

Dr. Nussbaum recommended a neurosurgeon to us
last week, and my heart galloped after Dr. Heros said,
in his Cuban accent, that he'd perform the surgery.
But ten minutes after hanging up the phone, I was
back to feeling empty. We decided on a date, September 13—my father purchased plane tickets to Miami
and made reservations at a hotel near Jackson Memorial. I couldn't find the words to tell him that none of
it will matter—that they should save their money for
the funeral. When I try to speak about how I'm feel-

ing my face flushes and a fist knocks inside my throat.

It doesn't matter what I do. I will fill with blood until my body can hold no more and burst, or I'll die after they split my head open.

Shivering, I snap a fistful of weeds from the ditch and then whip it into the wind, where the mess vanishes. I put my shorts on and stumble about, then drop to the gravel road. Facedown in the rutted mud, my body raw with sadness, I cry.

I want to rupture into a gasp of sorrowful ash because of everything I am. For fucking over my friends and the girls I pushed down in the backseats of Buicks, the girls I unzipped. The ones I've told to leave and then treated like shit. Each sip and puff and snort and chew. Pull after pull after pull. For each face I've kissed and punched and kicked and wept on. These fists. This throat. The way I've held a knife in front of me and how I've wrapped my hands around necks. For each thrust. The crack and crumble of ribs. For there is no changing that illbeat in my chest. For how Ma's face reddens when she cries. How my cousin pointed a knife at me after he was done and threatened the people I love, and how I told. For the many ways I've bled. For how Ma cries while I walk by the window. For not being brave enough to end it myself.

I kick my leg over the bike seat and wait for the strength to pedal home. The darkness bangs and fizzes when I close my eyes; a zipper gleams—like teeth, like the head of a penis, like a knife pushing into a body. It doesn't matter what I do now, it doesn't matter that I'm flying to Florida in September. I'm going to die.

"I'm leaving, Ma," I say when I walk in. Fanning herself with a magazine, her face contorts confusedly. She reaches for her glass.

"What?" she asks after taking a long drink. "What are you talking about?"

"I need to go." I'm filthy, still shaking from crying all afternoon.

"What are you talking about, Al?"

"I'm going to leave. I'm going on a trip."

"OK, Al," she laughs, like I'm teasing.

"Serious. I'm leaving." When I say it her face grims. She sets the glass down.

"I'm not sure that's a good idea, Ali. Don't you think you should stick around until we leave for Florida?"

"I'm leaving, Ma." There's nothing left for me to do here. "I'm going to Seattle to see Yarrow when she gets back from Thailand. I'm gonna ask Brown to go with me. I have to leave. I have to. I'll meet you in the Twin Cities for the flight."

"Shit, Al." She stares at me, rolls up *The New Yorker*, and slaps the armrest. "Don't you think you should take it easy? You should be resting, getting ready. Can I do anything?"

"Nope. I gotta go." I mutter, "I'm fucking out of here."

VIII

1

Two Days Later

"HOLY SHIT, AL! MOTHERFUCKING DEEEZ NUTS!" BROWN cackles when he answers the door. I've only seen him a couple of times since high school and he's more grown-up than I remember. A little Jesus beard. Broad shouldered and sunburned from roofing. We laugh and hug.

"What the fuck's happening, Lem?" He ruffles my hair and jumps down the steps. "Damn, G! Great to see you!"

"Yeah, man." I smile; I'd forgotten how much I love being around him. "I'm kinda—"

"Let's shoot the rock." Brown whoops, and grabs the basketball off the front lawn, streaks into the driveway, and starts taking frantic shots. The fourth one bounces around the rim. "CASH!" he shouts as it drops through the net. "I'm money."

I laugh and clap while he sticks his tongue out and dribbles, posts up an imaginary defender, and then hooks a shot off the front of the rim. "I still got game," he roars, snagging the rebound, banging in a layup. "So don't think you can bring your Gangja Martin shit in here. This is my house, bitch!"

He passes me the ball and I shoot a three from the street that knuckles through the air. "I'm fucking terrible," I laugh, chasing after the miss.

"Yes. Terrible, terrible. Terrible is right! But how the fuck are you, Al?" Grimacing like someone kicked him in the balls, he throws his elbows through the air, then hooks another layup in. "What you been up to, man?"

"Living with Ma for the summer."

"How's that going for ya?" He sneers and drop-kicks the ball, straight up in the air, and then points at his house with both arms like he's directing airplane traffic. "Don't you fucking *love* living at home? *Fuuuuuuccckk!* Shit, Al, I almost like going to work."

"Yeah, man. I'm not sure how it's going."

"What's up?" He picks the ball up, then overhands it at me like he's pitching a baseball. "Let's go, Gangja! Make it rain, motherfucker!"

It feels like I have a birdhouse in my throat when I talk. "Man. I don't know what's going on."

He hollers, *"Deeeez nuuuuutsss!!!"* as my shot arcs through the air and misses the rim by two feet. Before it hits the pavement he's shouting, *"Aiiiiirrr baaaaaaallllll!"* in the same tone.

"Remember that brain thing I had a couple of years ago? That shit everyone said was a fluke?" He frowns, quiet, and we sit in the driveway and I tell him I'm having brain surgery. It feels like I'm filling with blood, and no matter what I do, I think I'm going to die. "It's the end, dude! All she wrote!" I speak woodenly, tell him I'm going to Seattle to pick up Yarrow. "This is the big one! Road trip, man. You wanna go? Probably be my last one." I smile.

I wave at his father, who's standing behind the living room window, watching us. Dan grins and shakes his cane at us, then waves us in.

"Sure." Brown doesn't think about it. "You don't need to ask, Al. Come on, man! Let's tell my parents. Give me ten minutes to pack some shit, and I need to quit my job."

"Yeah?" I smile and he nods again.

When Ma and I moved to Iowa Falls, I walked to school alone the first day of eighth grade. I stood in front of River Bend Middle School by myself, kicking my shoes when kids looked at me. Brown jogged over, said, "Hey, what's your name?" and then asked if I was excited about being the new kid in a shitty town. At his house that night, Dan told me to pull up a chair and Cynthia asked if I'd stay for dinner.

TRUCKING NORTH ON I-35 A HALF HOUR LATER, WE'RE laughing frenziedly, talking about the night Brown took a shit on the windshield of Megan's car. The way it sludged down the glass in the blue light drifting from the house. "My fucking legs are tired," he had whispered, trying not to laugh, before pulling his shorts up.

"Can you believe we were cheerleaders?" Brown shouts over the stereo, ashing out the window. His long hair is tornadic and he's smiling. "Jeeezuz, do you remember that shit? What the hell were we thinking about?"

"Our friends' girlfriends' asses," I laugh. "If I remember right."

"Man, it's good to see you."

He puts Elton John's "Saturday Night's Alright for Fighting" into the CD player and I seal up the car. We shake our heads and laugh and in the cool truck cab, he rolls a joint.

The cornfields along I-90 in southwest Minnesota turn into great blankets of South Dakota sunflowers just past the state line. After an hour of quiet sunshine, I turn to him and frown. "Brown, I really think I'm going to die."

"Shit. Al, you think so?" He stops digging through my backpack, pulls out a bottle of vitamins, and rests them on the dash.

"Yep. Feel it in my gut. Remember how when you came home late or fucked up or whatever, and driving down the block you just knew you were going to be in deep shit? That your parents were waiting? You just knew it was going to be fucked and then it all happened just like you thought it would. It's like that."

"But you're taking all of these," he laughs, and then chucks the vitamin bottle over his shoulder and it smashes against the back glass. He mumbles, "Sorry."

"Fuck it."

"That sucks, Al." He starts nibbling some of the scattered pills. "All of the stupid shit we did that never went wrong. Fuck this brain stuff."

"Shit, man. No one's died yet. None of our friends. It's like a statistical fact, man. It's got to happen. It's math."

"I fucking hate going to funerals," he says after a minute of watching the pavement. "Bake my ass. Roll me up and smoke me!"

"Don't worry. You and Willie Nelson's beard."

"Fucking headband Willie!" He quiets, then asks "Really?" again.

"Dude. I feel all rotted inside."

"Man, Al, I'm fucking bummed."

He lights a smoke and cracks two beers and then hands me a bottle.

"But shit, man. I've had a fucking blast." I laugh and swig, and then smile at him. "So long!" I wave at the blurred freeway.

South Dakota is a bedlam of light as we drive into the sunset. I turn the radio back on. Brown rat-a-tats over the dashboard and then drumrolls the air. I will never figure out how to say good-bye to him.

NIGHT FALLS SYRUPY AND BLACK AROUND THE TRUCK. WHEN it starts raining, each exit sign flashes in the dark, filling the world with a sudden light. My vision bounces even worse because of the deluge, and the freeway dissolves in the headlights. I'm rigid and blind. I do not look away from the road.

Brown is talking about getting his driver's license revoked when the first motorcycle roars by. And then instantly, packs of the deafening Harley-Davidsons surround us. Thundering bikes are everywhere. The windshield is a sheet of water. The bikes flit between lanes, and I glance at Brown, wondering if I've started to hallucinate. Rain comes down so hard there isn't any spray from the Harleys' back wheels. There is only darkness. Red taillights when the bikes rumble by.

"Going kinda slow, buddy," Brown chuckles, and turns up the stereo.

I groan when I look at the speedometer—the truck is just creeping along. I'm too fucked up, trying to stay on the road. I lean forward and wait for one of the bikes to go down and crunch beneath us.

For an hour the interstate swerves with motorcycles.

"Al!" I jump when he says my name. "FIGURED IT OUT! It's fucking Sturgis, man," he howls blissfully. "Sturgis, man! Fucking Hell's Angels and shit."

"This is not good. Fuck this."

"Let's go to Sturgis, Al!" Brown laughs. "Let's stop! Let's do it up!"

Wipers arc across the windshield and taillights throb

into the night. The bikers wear sunglasses in the dark and the noise is brutal.

"Shut the fuck up." I turn off the stereo. "Come on, man."

Brown is gleeful, sings. "YEEEEAAAAAAAAAHHH!"

"Please?" I hunch over the wheel. "I'm fucking concentrating here."

BROWN IS ASLEEP, FACE MASHED AGAINST THE PASSENGER window, when I wake. A little boy stomps through a puddle. I don't remember how we got to this rest stop. Brown talks in his sleep while I have a chew and watch a man stretching next to his Toyota. I write good-bye letters in my journal until my hand hurts. The cab of the Silverado smells like a sewer so I get out and walk around the bathrooms and call Ma to tell her I'm OK. I hold the cigarette away from the phone while she talks.

Jumping back in the truck, I kick a bottle into the gas pedal and Fat Tire drains out on the floor mat. When I swear. Brown wakes and looks slowly around. He pinches his chin ponderously and stares out the windshield. "Yep, you sure did." He answers a question no one asked. "You freaked out last night, Al. You did!" He laughs groggily, pulls his Green Bay Packers stocking hat off, and wings it off the glass. He punches me in the shoulder and grins. "Freaking freak out, man! You think you're up to driving? I don't have no license, but shit, I'm game!"

"I'm awesome, thanks. But very funny," I laugh, and fire up the engine. "Freaking out!" I yell. "Let's freak out!"

Brown waves to the rest stop, starts throwing empty bottles out of the window, and then kicks his feet up on the dash.

AT THE TOP OF A TRAIL IN BEAVER NATIONAL FOREST we lounge around a mountain lake. Rocks bake in the sun, but discs of ice float in the shade. Gnats and water skimmers. A haggard-bare pine dying in the sun-bleached mud. Brown lays on a boulder, listening to his toaster-sized tape deck. He and Ma are the only people I know who still listen to cassettes. Skipping stones, I watch the tape player slide from his side into the lake, whipping the headphones into the rocks. He sits up like a movie-vampire, looks around confusedly, and then barks, "What the hell was that?"

Underwater, the tape plays on—normal at first, singing up from the muddy bottom, then slower and slower until it clicks off.

LATER THAT WEEK, WE DRIVE INTO THE HOH NATIONAL RAIN Forest and each radio station has news about a missing hiker who was last seen close to where we'd planned on camping. It'd rained the three days we crashed at Brown's brother's, and it's only gotten shittier and rain-gloomed since we left Olympia.

Happy

"No one cares!" Brown shouts over the news reports. "NO ONE! This is the best shit," he laughs after settling on some shreddy rock 'n' roll.

When the rain stops we roll the windows down and head-bang and scream lyrics at the vertebral trees. "Look What the Cat Dragged In." "Slave to the Grind." "Dirty Deeds Done Dirt Cheap." He puts in Guns N' Roses and Axl Roses from side to side, singing "Sweet Child O' Mine." He clicks the CD back and blasts "Welcome to the Jungle." It's so loud the humid air stings my face.

"Where the hos at!?" He yells into the dripping woods, reaches over to honk the horn. The forest hangs over the narrow road like a green, pounded sky. Rain purses from the trees. Pearls of light dangle from the leaves.

We pass two women on the muddy trail who make disgusted faces at each other after seeing how filthy Brown is. When they're out of hearing distance I hoot. "Oh shit, man. Did you see that look?" Rain is hammering through the trees again. "Did you see her face?" I yell and yell, but Brown doesn't turn back. Around us, the mossy labyrinth shakes. Lichen and leaves. Puddles sprawl across the trail.

"Time to catch our breath." He turns around, smiles, and lights a cigarette. His chin and mouth are splattered with mud. The gigantic yellow rain slicker he's wearing is just a plastic sheet with a head hole.

The torrential rain accentuates the lump his sleeping bag makes beneath it. He looks enormous, like I've been following the fucking sun through the rain forest. "I love nature," he says, handing me the pack of Winstons. "No bull," he laughs. "Fuckin' love it. All green and shit."

I'm bone-soaked and exhausted that afternoon when we make it to our campsite. Brown shivers palely, stocking hat so waterlogged his head turtles into his body. The tent my father got me collapses repeatedly, so we quit working, and, huddling in a dry spot, smoke weed and drink and eat granola bars. Hours later, somehow, the tent is up.

The camp stove shoots flames into Brown's face when it starts up and he shrieks "Fuck it" and chucks it into the brush. Eating uncooked food and cussing through my protests, he swears that his eyebrows were scorched off.

"We're like the fucking Beverly Hillbillies," I laugh, cracking open a beer, looking through the stuff we lugged out. Long underwear and socks hang from an elastic hoop inside the tent. Wet boots and open soup cans and beers and a dozen different wrappers are shrapneled around the campsite. "What is all this shit? Fuck, I need to go for a walk, man, I need some air."

"Don't have too much fun," he laughs.

After stumbling through the woods for twenty minutes, the tree canopy opens to a valley and the setting sun. The sky is purple in the east. The horizon is blazing in the west. Light quicksilvers over the creek in front of me. In the darkening light, I teeter on the water's edge. And then, just as the sun is about to vanish, for a moment, everything around me goes orange. The snowy peaks above the forest ripple brightly. The fading sun seems to fill the sky from horizon to horizon, weaving through the trees and rocks and river and dirt—orange orange orange, all at once. I crawl into the creek's cold glacier water as night inks and shadows and falls.

The woods are pitch-black and the tent is puffy with smoke when I get back. Brown is sitting in his underwear, finger-shoveling a can of beans into his mouth. He smiles, drinks from it. "Come in, dude," he gurgles. "Come in!" He holds the can out and the wet tin glints in the bluish dark. "You want some?"

"We have to hang the food because of bears. There was a sign at the trailhead."

"No, no, no, Al. Welcome! Come in! Beans!"

"The stuff, man. Bears."

"Fuck the bears," he says. "We need the food right here. We are hungry people."

"Hellooooohelllllooooooo!" someone yells out in the forest in the middle of the night, and suddenly, I'm wide awake. Footsteps crack through the twigs. Brown clicks on the flashlight and asks if I'm up. For a minute, the woods are still, and then, again, the long *hellos* come. The woods swish and groan. There are heavy boots outside and a man breathes "Hello." A fist knocks against the tent, boinging condensation down on us.

"Yeah. Howdy? Can we help you?" I ask.

"Who goes there?" Brown snickers.

"Hi. I hope I didn't startle you. I wanted to ask a few questions." Brown and I poke our heads out of the tent. I try not to stare while the man introduces himself but he has big sick eyes and a trucker mustache. A knife on his belt. "I'm part of a group of forest workers looking for a missing man. I'm not sure if you've heard."

"THAT DUDE WANTED TO FRY UP OUR GENITALS AND EAT 'EM," Brown laughs after the guy leaves. He holds the flashlight under his chin. "Get all Dahmer on us."

"Did you see him licking his lips?" I laugh, but the man totally creeped me out. I pocket my trembling hands.

"Sweet dreams! Muhahahahaa!" Humid smoke fills the tent, thick as bread, as the lighter flicks. He passes it, and I smoke up and mummy myself in the sleeping bag.

I'm awake for hours, listening to the forest bleed, waiting for the man to come back with his knife. The woods cloister and rasp. Tightly bound in a sleeping bag I never gave back to Julie, I think about never being able to say sorry to everyone I want to. Killing my cousin. I practice my good-bye letters in my head and cry, dreaming about the things I'll never be able to do.

Laughing uncomfortably and scratching our heads in the morning, we decide we've had enough. We pack up all of our shit and hike back to the truck.

"WHAT A FUCKING AWESOME TRIP, MAN." I STARE AT THE road and sip coffee. The sky is gray; Olympia is windy and cold. I'm dropping Brown off at his brother Tim's; in a couple of weeks, he's going to find a way back to Iowa. "Oh, shit, I like this one." I turn up the Red Hot Chili Peppers, ignoring the sick billowing in my guts. Street signs wobble. Tree limbs stab the peppery air.

At the stoplight, two blocks from Tim's, I mute the stereo. In front of the windshield, a spray of birds is flapping madly, like puppets hanging from the sky. "I wanted to thank you, man. You know, like . . . I had an amazing time. Pretty fucking great. Thanks."

Parked on the empty street, I look at him, but he's staring at Tim's house.

"Shit, Al," he says, opening the door. "No need, brother. Good times, man. We'll do it again."

I stand in the gravel next to the truck, hands hanging like sandbags at my sides. Instead of telling him I don't think we will, I cry.

"Fucking good times, Al." We hug for five minutes, and when I stand back, his face is teary and smiling.

"OK, I have to go, Browntown. Lots of bullshit I

gotta do, you know?" I grin and wipe my eyes. "Gotta get some shit done! I love you, man."

"Love you too, Al."

The Silverado fishtails over the slick road. My coffee spills when the tires squeal.

2

I'M BEWILDERED WHEN I SEE YARROW AT THE AIRPORT. SHE'S been in Thailand all summer and so much has happened. She's like a visitor from another life, and I'd forgotten how magnificent she is. She looks like a young Lauren Hutton, just prettier and muscled from running miles each day under the Thai sun. She's blonder than she was, a flower behind her ear, with freckles laid out over her cheeks. It smells like citrus oils when she leaps into the truck. She gives me a necklace sewn of small roses and my insides tighten, then go vacant as I smile. She crosses and uncrosses her legs, moves closer, and asks if I missed her. I nod and we kiss, but after a few seconds of touching, we break apart, laughing because it's been too long and our mouths are new again and awkward.

IN BELLINGHAM THE FOLLOWING WEEK, WE SPEND DAYS like we did last year at college. She hadn't yet transferred to Mac when I had the first brain hemorrhage, and we've hardly discussed it, so I don't talk to her about it. Nothing I'm thinking about is said out loud—the numbness in my body, my clumsiness and dread—though we both know I'm leaving for Florida soon. We run the trail around a lake and I ignore the way my eyes bounce but tell her to go ahead without me. I have to rest because I'm afraid I'm going to fall. I sit on a log with my head in my hands. She passes every fifteen minutes. We go on hikes and I stumble even though I'm using hiking poles now. I ignore how I couldn't feel my face all day. I grip tree limbs when we stop for a drink of water. One morning, Yarrow, her father, her stepmom, and I hike together. Standing ankle-deep in sun-gleaming snow, they rub herbs into my limbs and chest and chant, but it doesn't mean anything to me. I can't feel it. With my numb face, the mountaintop wind is no different than a rope burn or Yarrow's breath after a kiss. It all feels the same now.

Yarrow and I laugh and eat avocados and cream cheese and mangoes and read poems aloud under candlelight. In my sleepless hours after we make love, I have to stop myself from pushing her awake, asking if she feels anything, anything at all, when I touch her.

On the drive back to Minnesota with Yarrow, I take hundreds of pictures. Our feet pressed against the windshield. Pavement, sidewalks, highway, interstate. Loan ads on park benches and the clear blue sky. The speedometer at a hundred miles per hour, the gas on E.

Yarrow's profile. Eating something hot. Frown-faced. Eating something delicious. Blowing a kiss. In love. Thinking about Nebraska. Russet hills held down by a hand. Thinking about Iowa. Angry. Smiling. Confused. I hold the camera to the side and take snapshots when we're seated in restaurants. Silos and barns and graffitied trains. Rusted cars at Mobil stations. Kum and Go. I take shots of the moon while she sleeps next to me. I shoot roll after roll of film, and then, driving all night while Yarrow sleeps, I splice the images in my head—the perfect stills in which nothing is ever wrong, all of that surface and sheen. She wakes, yelps "Whoa!" when the truck jerks over the shoulder of the road and then back, but she doesn't ask why I keep spacing out.

Yarrow and I make love when we get back to St. Paul, and then she goes for a run. I lie in bed, my packed bags next to me. I'm flying to Miami in the morning. I listen to reports of a tropical storm forming in the Atlantic Ocean, east of Africa. There's a good chance its path will take it to Florida.

That night is a film reel of faces. I don't want to see anyone, but my friends have made other plans; everyone wants to say good-bye. At Dan's house, I hand out the gifts Ma's made for my friends: stickers and T-shirts and buttons with images she's Photoshopped— my baby pictures backdropped with constellations. I joke about it to lighten the mood but tell them what

Ma wanted me to say, that they should wear them on September 13.

We drink wine and beers and they smoke pot and I cry when they hold me, but as the night goes on I get tired and angrier—I'm so sick of smiling. Tomorrow, I'll be in an airplane over Alabama when they wake half-drunk and decide that they don't need to go to class.

After going to campus to see more people, I walk to Casey's apartment on Grand. I didn't call him all summer and just recently told him what was going on. On the stoop we slap hands and hug. My fingers don't feel like mine when I raise the cigarette to my lips.

"I'm not good at this." I wisp out the smoke. "I'm fucking exhausted."

"Yeah, man. I hear you."

"Sorry I didn't call."

The cigarette makes his face glow and I can tell he's not pissed at me; he's sad. No matter how much we try to out-tough each other and bullshit, he's still my best friend.

"Don't sweat it, Al. It's cool." He twists out the butt and stands in the humid night.

"I'm sick of talking, Case."

"No worries." He laughs and cracks his thumb knuckles in his palms.

I hug him again and leave.

IX

1

September 9, 1999

I'VE NEVER LONGED FOR SNOW AS MUCH AS I DO WHEN WE step out of the airport in Miami. It's sweltering and asthmatic: light honeycombs languidly through the palm trees. As I pack luggage into the trunk of the rental car, sweat runs down my face like I just climbed out of a swimming pool.

Ma was silent on the plane. Dad pointed out magazine articles he thought I'd like and Lindy read about Russian czars. My parents get along better than they used to, but when all of us are together I feel like a dancing monkey, trying to entertain the crowd, grinning at their heavy eyes. I smiled and then pretended to sleep, hoping the plane would explode.

As THE SUN SETS I TELL MA THAT I'M GOING TO WALK around until the four of us go to dinner and then

stand on the motel balcony and listen to my Disc-
man. She and I are sharing a room. Dad and Lindy
are in one on the floor above us. A razor-wire security gate fences in the parking lot: video cameras are
perched at the entrance. I inhale the raw-potato
smell of the ocean, the fumes from the cleaning cart
that's been sitting on the walkway all day. When the
wind dies, exhaust from passing cars is overpowering. Across the street and a few blocks away, the
Jackson Memorial medical complex looks like a for-
tress. I'm meeting the neurosurgeon for the first time
tomorrow afternoon. Just a few more days, and I'll
be checking in.

"Don't eat that," Ma says as I raise a fork of cheesecake to my lips. Dad and Lindy stop talking, look up
from their desserts. The bay wind flickers the candlelight. Waves lap against the pier's pilings below us. I
stare at Ma.

"Whatever," I say derisively. "I can eat what I want,
Ma."

She slowly napkins her mouth, then sighs and drops
the cloth onto her plate. I plop the bite into my mouth
dramatically and grin, then squeegee up the leftover
whipped cream with my index finger.

Walking back to the car, I try to ditch my parents
in the pier's carnival games and rides. A mosaic of
lights bling in the crowd. I randomly turn around
hoop-tossing games and lines of ticket holders, but

when I look up again, there my family is, waiting at each curb.

When I get back to our room after saying good night to Dad and Lindy, Ma's pulled off the two bedspreads. The pastel blankets are mounded on the floor. Standing between the mattresses, she talks on the phone and flips through channels, jabbing the remote at the TV.

I try to read, but each time I finish a line of words my vision skips down three or four lines, so I climb from the bed and do push-ups on the floor.

"Bob says he loves you," she says after hanging up.

"He's coming down on Tuesday, right?" I strain up and down, then turn over and do leg lifts.

"Yep." She nods without looking from the television. Growing up, we never had a TV, and she always jokes that we need to get our money's worth when we're in hotels, so usually, we stay up all night watching cable. "A thousand channels and nothing good, Ali. What a bunch of shit." But she keeps staring.

"You are dead to me, TV," she says, turning it off fifteen minutes later. The remote lands beside me, and she kicks through the bedspreads on her way to the bathroom. "Ali, they never wash those, you know? So don't touch 'em unless you want herpes or impetigo. Remember when you had ringworm?" she laughs. "Wrapped your head up like a mummy." She's still talking about how filthy motel blankets are when the door closes and the shower turns on.

I'm half-asleep when Ma comes out, folds the sheets

down, and exhales onto her bed. The TV turns on, and she drinks carbonated water, belching quietly. I didn't realize how tired I was until I slid into bed; being around my parents stresses me the fuck out.

"It was moldy," Ma says, brushing her hair in the dim room. She grabs the remote from the table and clicks up the volume. "Nasty shit."

"What?" I groan, roll so I'm not facing her. "I was sleeping, Ma. Jesus, I need to get some rest. You said I needed to rest."

"At dinner . . . Your cheesecake," she says absent-mindedly. "I was trying to tell you that the cheesecake was moldy. Probably didn't taste that good, huh?"

"Buckle up!" Dad laughs in the morning when I sit down in the lobby. He hands me the newspaper; the front page has a satellite picture of the tropical storm they've named Floyd. "This could get interesting . . . Alex, where's your mother?"

"She's going to catch up to us when we meet the doctor," I say, scanning the article. The storm is monstrous and gaining speed—it has the potential to be one of the biggest hurricanes in U.S. history, and it's supposed to make landfall on the Florida coast next week.

"What the shit is this?" I toss the paper back to him.

"Batten down the hatches!" He grins and slaps my knee. "Might be a bumpy ride!"

Happy

Dad talks to the guy at the front desk and calls the hospital to get more information. If the storm stays on course, it could be trouble. There's already talk about evacuations.

Dr. Heros glides through his office at the U of Miami like a retired pro basketball player. He looks into our eyes as he shakes each of our hands and asks us to sit. He emigrated from Cuba, became a U.S. paratrooper, and was held captive for two years after the Bay of Pigs invasion, but there's not a hint of violence in him. He's olive-skinned and tall, pressing his suave tie down.

When we sit, he smiles and then cuts to the chase. He describes the surgery and walks behind me and presses my head forward. His hands are smooth, pattering over my skull and neck and back. When his warm hands tilt my chin down, I get tunnel vision.

"You're in good shape," he says, running a finger down my neck. "This is helpful. It will help your recovery. It's very good."

I'll be facedown in something like a massage chair during the procedure. After I'm fully sedated and under, the medical team will make the incision on my neck and then splay open the neck and head skin. Using digital enhancement and previous images of the pooling blood, they'll cut at an angle, slightly shift the good brain tissue so that they can get at the brain stem without having to remove any of my skull. His hand angles down like a crashing airplane. If the malformation is near the surface of the pons, they'll remove it. If it goes well, he says, the surgery will take ten hours.

Dr. Heros looks directly at me.

"But if the lesion is too deep, if there is too much live tissue to cut through, I will not be able to do anything. I do not want to risk it. Alex, that is something you must consider before you agree to this. If that is the case, if I'm not comfortable removing the malformation, we will have to close you back up, and then, when you've recovered, everyone will hope for the best."

Without blinking, he eloquently answers my parents' questions. Any surgery this deep in the brain is risky. The procedure might go perfectly, and very little, if anything at all, could be wrong with me. With these surgeries there is always the possibility of death. The brain stem is critical to life, and just getting to it is a medical challenge. There is a chance that the surgical team might not be able to remove the entire lesion, and I might continue having aneurisms. Even if the surgery is successful, there is a likelihood of neurological and/or physical deficits. The deficits run the gamut; no one will know the range and extent of them until the days and weeks after I wake.

Everyone clears their throat at the same time, and then the room quiets.

I want to puddle into the floor, but I can't stop staring at Dr. Heros's hands, how they flutter, fold, and weave while he speaks.

Happy

"In the end, this is all up to you," he says. "I hope you feel well informed. It's your choice, Alex. It's up to you."

I nod and lie—*I understand everything*. I sign my name on the release form and then lean back in the chair while Dr. Heros talks about the coming storm.

At breakfast in a café on Ocean Drive the next morning, my parents talk worriedly about how large Floyd has gotten. Yesterday it turned into a hurricane and was moving through the Caribbean. On the news, tropical storm and hurricane warnings are being announced every ten minutes. I sip orange juice and watch a wrinkled man smoke outside the window. His hands shake, and he ashes on himself and then swipes the soot down his shirt. My pancakes are tasteless, so I excuse myself and sit in the bathroom.

Dad and Lindy want to shop, so after eating, we plan to meet later and then split up.

The sky is Prussian blue and flamed with clouds while Ma and I sand-kick down Lummus Beach. She watches from the shore as I wander into the waves and pluck shells from the clear water. I dip my entire arm in and sift through the sand. I dunk my head and wave at her. When I trudge back, Ma hands me an empty Styrofoam cup. The top half of it looks like it's been chewed apart by rats.

"You got some good ones," she says after we sit,

shells fanned out in front of us, drying in the sun. She finger-dusts sand off of them and polishes them with spit and her shirt.

"Yeah, they're OK, I guess." I hold up a cracked whelk. "Most of 'em are busted, though."

"Still, Ali. Some good ones."

And then, for a long time, we don't talk. Ma digs a trough and it slowly fills with water. I stare out at the ocean while she surrounds her tiny lake with igloo-shaped mounds. Families pass where we're sprawled. Bodybuilders swagger by, flexing their pecs. A woman in a white G-string walks by and I gawk and Ma shakes her head. Far out on the ocean, shipping tankers domino the hem of the water. The horizon is dark gray and rolling black.

When we stand, plunking the shells into the cup, the sky looks like a chalkboard. It's cooler now. The wind gusts. Ma is flagging sand from her hair when a tan little girl slides to a stop in front of us. She is a giant smile with black hair and tiny bones.

"Have mine, too," she says, looking at me. "You take them." The bowl of her hands overflows with shells.

Seagulls swing and plunge through the air above the shallows.

"They're for you." She reaches the shells out. "You have them."

"What?" I say, staggered.

"For you."

"Why?"

Happy

"Just 'cause," she says happily. She's probably ten years old. "You should have 'em. They're good."

Ma squeezes an arm around my waist and pulls me close.

"Are you sure?" I wheeze. Each of the shells is immaculate, the kind tourists pay good money for. "Don't you want to keep them?"

She shakes her head from side to side fiercely, and her tangle of hair glints and whips in the whirling sand.

"Thank you," Ma says, and then looks at me.

I nod and smile. "Yeah, thanks."

The girl grins, drops the shells in our dirty cup, and scampers down the beach.

BEAUTIFUL PEOPLE MILL THROUGH THE RESTAURANT: smiles and sun-darkened skin levitate around us. I eat salad croutons, cut my steak into chunks so small I don't have to chew to get them down, and drink Heinekens. Our table is so quiet, my swallows sound like cannon blasts.

I'm supposed to check into the hospital tomorrow night so the surgical team can start prepping me. At six on Monday morning, a nurse will come to my room. Final preparations will take two hours. If all goes according to plan, Dr. Heros said, the surgery will start at eight A.M.

It's all I can think about at dinner with Dad and Lindy. I nod and smile, but I can't get it out of my head.

"You got cooked today," Dad says.

"Don't you worry." Lindy smiles. "I'll get you some lotion."

Dad presses his fingers into my sunburned forearm, and when he lets go, my arm has two blankwhite eyes.

MA GIBBERS IN HER SLEEP WHILE I WATCH TV; A WEATHER-man points at time-lapse images of the swirling hurricane. I turn the channel and a woman in a rain slicker is reporting from the beach. The next one I flip to has video of a ravaged town in the Caribbean, downed power lines, and police lights and chainsaws. A flashlight herkyjerkying through a caved-in home. Outside the motel, the wind brays like a hundred thousand cellists.

I do not dream of being saved from all of this. I do not dream of waking after the surgery, my family and doctors all smiles, high-fiving and saying things are fine. The dream I have is not the same dream I've been dreaming since my freshman year, the one where I murder everyone I love, shower in lighter fluid, then press a match to my lips.

I am buried in the mealwormed earth in the dream. The dirt is dank and hot and putrid. A caustic tang fills my mouth, and I swallow and gag on the rotten muck until there's room enough to claw. I scratch and dig until the skein above me grows light and I smell a bee garden. Sunlight wallops me when I break through the crust of soil. By the time I've clambered out of the hole, the ocean breeze has dried a suit of dirt over me. I stand, blinking and gasping in front of the motel's shining security gate. Fresh rain stretches gobby from the fence. When I turn, I'm facing the hurricane-destroyed motel. Smashed glass is spawned out at my feet, glittering neon and wet. And then I'm knee-deep in the ruins, yelling out my parents' names and screaming for Ma. I'm standing in the mess, tossing a ripped-in-half door to the side, when I wake.

HIDING OUT IN THE BATHROOM AFTER LUNCH, I CAN HEAR the downpour stop. All morning, the rain sounded like a convoy of passing semis, and then, while I had my head in my hands and checked my watch to see how long I'd been sitting on the toilet, it quit.

My father and Lindy and Ma are standing in the room when I come out. Peels from the oranges Ma and I ate are stacked pyramidal on the dresser. Ma squeezes a rind anxiously, zesting the air.

"They're closing the hospital because of the hurricane," my father says. "Everything's shutting down, so the surgery is off for now." I look at Lindy, then Ma, and then Dad. He's red-jowled, flexing his jaw. "People are evacuating Miami"—he starts dialing his cell phone—"and the counties around here. It's supposed to hit on Tuesday or early Wednesday. They're saying all sorts of crazy shit." He talks loudly into the phone and walks out of the room. The wind blasts the door against the wall.

The TV anchor lists items every household should have in preparation for a hurricane. A flashlight and a hand-cranked radio on the desk. Soup cans and bottled water. Smiling, he twists a manual can opener in his fist. There's video of jugs of water being yanked from grocery-store shelves, then the aisles of a Home Depot, crowds dragging away wall-sized sheets of plywood.

"As soon as they put it on the shelves," the reporter in front of the fracas says, "it's gone!" He grins. "Back to you!"

Dad comes back in, still talking, so I mute the TV. The man at the front desk said that we can stay in the motel if we want, but only minimal services will be provided. Most of the workers are going home. Airlines are starting to cancel flights in and out of Miami. On TV, thousands of cars are bumper to bumper, gridlocked on the freeways heading out of town.

"They are getting the hell out of here!" Dad chortles and shakes his head. "Ahhhh hell, what should we do?" He calls the hospital again; my surgery cannot be rescheduled until they know more about the hurricane.

Outside, the wind revs and pistons.

People are crying on TV. There are cops and press conferences and reporters and more weathermen. A list of words—HURRICANE ESSENTIALS—scrolls across the bottom of the screen. We sit speechless and watch, until I can open my mouth and say, "I think we should stay."

Happy

Lying in bed that night, I listen to windows being boarded up. Nail guns whop and gasp in the dark.

In the morning, there's a hesitating sprinkle on the balcony but no wind. The streets are deserted. The pigeons that had been pecking at popcorn on the walkway each day we've been here are gone. Two cars in the motel parking lot; the security gate is wide open. The rain stops while I talk to Yarrow on a pay phone. The boulevard's palm trees slump lazily. No water falls from the lowering sky.

Dad mutes the TV when I stop by their room and shows me the piece of paper someone slipped under the door. Emergency phone numbers on one side, a bulleted list of directives beneath "Surviving a Hurricane" on the other. "You sure you want to stay?" he asks. "We still have a little time."

I tell him I want to stay.

Ma and I walk the vacant streets. Yoo-hoo-colored water fills the ditches, and trash grips the fences. An empty Coca-Cola can tinkles across the sidewalk. After we've been meandering quietly for hours, miles from the motel, Ma smiles up at me, and I think we must be lost—the downtown luster has been replaced by paint-chipped dilapidation and all of the signs are in Spanish. The Jackson Memorial complex glowers in the distance, but the homes we pass are broken-windowed and run-down. I want to turn back, but Ma says we need to go to a store she found the other day. She pulls me forward, points, says, "It's right up here."

Old cars are parked cockeyed up and down the street in front of the decrepit storefront. The vehicles are all empty but some have their headlights on. The windshield wipers on a double-parked pickup go back and forth even though it hasn't rained in hours.

A woman backs out of the bodega with bags draped down her arms, skin pinched like the plastic is loaded with gravel. I hold the door for the two men who follow her. Ma and I walk in and people are shoulder-to-shoulder in the tight aisles, grabbing the few items still on the shelves. No one looks at us, but I get anxious because we're the only white folks there. Ma pushes her way in. This happened every trip we took when I was young. Ma never seemed afraid; if there was something we *needed* to see, she'd drag me into places everyone said were unsafe—the Watts Towers; East St. Louis; the desert outside of Vegas, by the whorehouses and nuke sites. I watch the top of her white hair bob down an aisle until she vanishes. Everyone in the market is yelling in Spanish, knocking shopping carts and baskets. Two TVs are on different channels. A radio plays full volume next to the clerk. The static of one in the back drifts through the tumult. I wander into the crowd, then turn and stare at a stained-glass picture of a rooster on the wall. Shoppers flow around me, floating me back and forth over the sticky floor.

A half hour later, Ma emerges from the wall of people and asks if I'm ready to go. Nine customers have paid and walked out the bonging door while I stood next to the counter like a statue. "You not getting nuthin'?" She looks at my empty hands, says, "I'm buying."

"Don't need anything." I sigh. "Let's go."

She skips to the end of the line. "Don't be sorry later." When it's Ma's turn, she says "Hello," stretching the O into an *ooooooooooh*, and sets a chocolate bar and a candle down and asks for two extra bags. The man finger-punches the register, speaks to Ma in Spanish as he bags. Ma shakes her head, says, "Two more bags, please?" and he repeats himself in Spanish, slowly. A woman behind us exhales as Ma holds her cash out to him, bills fanned apart like a straight flush. When the clerk tries to wrestle some of the money away, Ma holds on, letting him tug. I'm embarrassed, about to go outside, but Ma smiles at me and then releases the dollars. The grocer's eyes light up, and he and Ma laugh. Grinning, he says "Have a nice day" in perfect English as Ma pockets her change. He holds open the bag-grip for Ma's wrist, then hands her two empty bags.

Leading us back to the motel, Ma holds my hand. We don't talk, and by the time we walk into the parking lot, we're wearing the extra bags like bonnets. The raindrops sound like firecrackers when they hit the crinkly plastic.

MA WAKES ME UP EARLY MONDAY MORNING, TOTALLY FREAK-ing out. It stormed most of the night, but it's stopped again. Sitting on my bed, Ma asks if I think Dr. Heros is boarding up his house by himself. I turn on the TV, and every station has hurricane news on. "Do you think he's on a ladder?" she asks. "Do you think he's doing it himself?" I shrug. On TV the surf crashes in great breakers over lifeguard stations. "He's probably got someone to do it for him, don't you think, Ali? He's not doing it, I'm sure of it." The camera pans down a block of oceanfront homes; each has boarded-up windows. Most of the plywood is graffitied. "I mean, he's got to protect his hands, right?" she asks. "He's got someone to help him, to do it for him. I bet he does." The radar image of Hurricane Floyd is massive. It's twice the size of Florida, rotating slowly, racing closer. "Don't you think? He's not doing it, right? He needs to think about you. Maybe I should do it," she says. "Maybe I should call and see if I can do it for him. I would do it for him. No problem. I should do it." The next station shows the same footage we saw last night, the flashlight searching through the wrecked house. "I'm gonna call, Ali. I'm gonna call him. Don't you think I should? You don't think he's doing it himself, do you?" The camera zooms in on a piece of plywood painted with WE LOVE YOU FLOYD! SPARE OUR HOME! The TV goes black and a commercial for McDonald's comes on. There is a press conference. The Broward County sheriff and the governor talk. The anchor says President Clinton is returning to the U.S. early, that he might declare Florida a disaster area before the hurricane even hits. "Ali, he's thinking about his hands, right? I'm gonna call. Don't ya think I should? I'll just call him. I'll do it. He needs to think about his hands, about you." Her worry is like a tire-fire in the small room. I turn off the TV, walk into the bathroom, and shut the door. It sounds like apples are falling from heaven when the rain starts again. Ma picks up the phone before it finishes the first ring. She says hello to my dad, tells him I'm not available, and then hangs up. In the shower I recite, *"Whatever happens. Whatever / what is is is what / I want. Only that. But that,"* until I'm mumbling a trainwreck of *whats* and *wants* and *ises.* I sob into the steam. When I turn the water off, wind is throttling everything.

AFTER WE WATCH THE WEATHERMAN SMILE THE HURRICANE turning from the Florida coast my brain stem malformation strokes bleeds quality of life the bloody mulberry a highly eloquent area the uncomfortable laughing because the hurricane didn't do anything at all only rain wind and more wind and rain the hospital opens and I leave everything in the motel room I check in at dusk not eating or drinking for twelve hours all night in my hospital room folding my jeans over the back of my hospital chair my T-shirt drops hooked up to an IV and I gawk at the ceiling the TV muted but blaring from down the hall the birds skitter rocks outside my window as night begins to orange and I look up to see Ma and Bob and Dad and Lindy it is morning and they are there terrified already grieving and I feel guilty for all of it and roll my IV with me to pee one last time my father says behind me is that a tattoo on his back I weep in the mirror then say good-bye the nurse asks me to sit in the wheelchair so she can take me away the good-bye clangs inside me and after being rolled away I'm hooked to more tubes and machines in the preparing hum of the operating room and the drip starts placing me just so and after *Would you move just a little to the left* after *The doctor likes it this cold* after *Can you feel this?* after *This is to make you a bit warmer* I don't get a chance to say I am wonderful under these streetlights just plain good screaming into the antiseptic air I'm so fucked this is the end thank you it's been a blast I love all you fucks or even as the dark bag of the anesthesia zippers me up get to whisper my welcome to the tumbling and crushing and delivering black.

2

Hello better dark. Solemn voices. Bodies swish in the beeping void. *Hello black world.* Everything hurts and I'm blind. *Hello perfect bruise.* I'm on my back. Moaning. My mouth is crammed full. Fingers. Tubes. Vomit. And I'm ice-cold. *Hello never again.* Just seconds ago the lights went out. *Hello hello hello—*

Someone caresses my head, and I garble, "Don't fucking touch me." My father's intake of breath. Fingers pull away when I scream.

Someone speaks. The dark answers *something over something.*

I retch when the tubes tear out of me. Saliva and blood and puke wax my face. The muck wells in my mouth. Down my throat. I choke until a hand turns my head. I heave. Again and again. Someone wipes the mess from my face. More tubes are whipped out of me.

This is not the afterlife I imagined.

LIGHT ZIGZAGS ABOVE ME WHEN MY VISION STARTS TO return, but I can't make sense of shit. There is just a hive of noise, an incessant thrum. I have nothing left to throw up but my body keeps convulsing.

"Who are you?" the light asks. "What year is it? Who is the president? Where are you? What's your name? What's your name?" Shadows move frantically.

I'm hooked up to more machines. Someone asks why my pulse is so slow. I try to tell them that I want the quiet and dark but I can't speak.

The brightness flickers, goes out. There are no more questions.

WHEN THE DARK BURNS AWAY, ALL I CAN SEE IS A VIVID SPAT-ter. The questions start again, unfurling a liquidy veil of sound. A warmth climbs and coils and sears up my arm and into my chest. It feels like a woodshop is working inside me—drill press and lathe and awl.

"Al." Spit rains over my face. "I am Alex."

The light asks who the president is, and I answer, "Bill Clinton. 1999. Bill fuckin' Clinton." The light wants more. It won't let me go. "This is Miami, and I am Alex." I beg, but the light does not stop. "Florida," I shout. "Why can't I see?" I ask, but the light doesn't answer, the light only asks. The light does not stop. Noise carousels above me; the world is filled with wind chimes. "Alex. Clinton. Miami," I say. The light spangles above. The room's beeps are eggs laid in my head and I can't see. It's a horrific kaleidoscope, brightness porcupining my face. "I am Al, and this is Florida, and I am Alex, and the president is Clinton." I yell, coughing up chunks of spit and vomit and blood. My face is shoved sideways again and before it goes black, I shout, "I am Al. Alex. Al. Shit. Miami, Florida. Shit. Clinton is president. And we're going to party like it is 1999."

EVERYTHING IS YOLKY WHEN I OPEN MY EYES. I CAN'T BLINK it away. The surgery must have failed. I'm lying in another bed, but my body doesn't do anything I want it to; I can't move. A voice says that I'm in the neurology intensive care unit. It keeps telling me to stay awake.

"A sip of water?" I ask, but it comes out guttural, as nonsense. My dried lips split when I beg. "Please?"

"What? Oh," the woman says, then. "Not yet," before moving away.

A clumping of feet rushes in and my family cries around me.

"I love you, Al," Ma says. She's inches from my face. "You are my baby. You are so, so strong."

"What a day, Alex," my father says, gripping my shoulder. "What a day." He laughs uncomfortably. "Looking good, son. My little Babaloo."

The family-shapes speak softly when they lean over

me: Ma and Dad and Bob and Lindy. The surgery didn't take the ten hours that Dr. Heros thought it would. He thinks it went well. The shadows squeeze my wrist and say they love me.

I'm trying to ask them to stay when I hear them walk out.

"ALEX, MY NAME IS MIGUEL," A VOICE SAYS BESIDE ME. "I'M going to be watching you tonight. All night. Call for me anytime. Push this if I'm away." He nestles a rectangle in my hands, then guides my fingers over a button.

The corners of my mouth tear when I breathe.

"Thanks." I gasp, excited that there's someone out there, that my mouth will finally make words. "Thank you."

"Not a problem." He sounds young. "It's my job," he laughs. "You need anything right now?"

"Some water? Please?"

"Not yet, Alex. I'm sorry. A while longer." His shape stands next to my bed for a moment before he goes to work. Clothes rustle. Buttons are pushed, and the bed moves beneath me. "Is that better?" he asks. "We'll get you all good." He touches the tubes in my arm, says a series of numbers out loud. There is tapping and writing, and then receding footsteps.

"HELLO?" I SAY, WAKING TERRIFIED WITH A SHAPE HANGING over me. It's right in front of me. I don't know how long I was out. "Miguel? That you?" I can feel the person staring at me. "Hello? Hello?"

"Just me." Miguel sighs and walks away. "I'll be right back, Alex."

He leans over me when he returns, pressing a damp sponge to my lips.

"Oh, man." It feels so good, I can't help it—I grin. "Thank you, Miguel. Thanks." I flick my tongue around my mouth and taste blood.

For hours, Miguel daubs my chapped skin and tells me stories about Miami. "The best in the world," he says about the dancing and women and clubs. He laughs. "If you like having a good time." His shoes dance and skittle and I imagine what he looks like. "Hey, Alex. Stay awake for a bit. You listening?"

"Yup." The drugs are wearing off and all of me hurts.

The sponge stops. "You want more for your lips?" he asks. "You good for now?"

My face stings dryly. Skin pulls off each time he touches my mouth. "Yeah, good. But I'm really thirsty."

"Sorry, Alex. You have to wait for a while. Head trauma. Doctors' rules." The chair slides on the tiles when he sits. It creaks. "So how did you get here? What happened?"

In just seconds, my lips are peeling again, swollen and strawberried. Struggling to remember my story, I tell him the last thing I heard: that Dr. Heros said the surgery went better than anyone could have expected.

"That's great news."

I want to ask why I can't see if I'm still alive, but I'm afraid I'll cry.

I WAKE SOME TIME LATER TO SOBBING — MACHINERY BEEPS and keens while voices scream, "*NOOOOOO!!!*" Footsteps stampede over the tiles.

"Hello?" I shout, but no one answers. I still can't see. "Hey, Miguel? You there?" I don't know if I fell asleep or what. I don't know what the fuck is going on. "Miguel? You there?" The ICU is dark now. Somewhere close, a computerized pulse whines and people are crying. There's screeching next door. I push the call button over and over but no one comes. "What is all that?" I yell, but there are only more hurrying footsteps and shouts. Wheels rolling over the tiles. The hospital's monstrous thrum.

"Hello? Miguel?"

It's flint black when I close my eyes. Now that I can move, I bury my hands beneath my ass and pretend that I haven't heard anything. That Miguel said he had to go piss. He'll be right back to wet my lips. I'm surrounded by beautiful singing, I say to myself; I can will myself to sleep.

Miguel is sighing heavily when he reaches toward me again. He says, "Hey," and runs the sponge over my mouth, faster than before, fraying it. And then he's missing my lips completely. The darkness is silent and lingering. There's no more bodytalk. No more bikinis or singing in Spanish. No shoes dancing while he works.

"This place sounds like a nightclub or something, right?" I ask. Miguel jerks the sponge away when I laugh.

"Emergency," he says. "Guy your age tried to make it through a train crossing on his motorcycle." Miguel pats my lips. He presses them harder, pokes one time, and then stops. "Didn't make it." Miguel stands and leans against the wall. His shape doesn't move for a long time.

3

When I wake on the sixth day I'm still shaky and sea-
sick—my tungsten-boned legs are frozen under the
bedsheets. My vision is muzzy now, but I can see that
there's no one in my hospital room. Sunlight filters
through the shades like they're made of gauze.

"Hey, hey! Where'd everybody go?" The words stick
and slur in my mouth. My head wobbles and then
tears from the pillow like masking tape. Each time I
fall asleep the incision dries to the cloth. My chin
droops to my chest, then rolls to the right. The pillows
Ma piled behind me slide out and one falls to the floor.
My head snaps and lolls. I'm a rag doll.

"Hello?" I yell. "Hello? . . . Awww, fuck y'all!"

When the doctors said that I was going to be OK
two days ago, everyone left but Ma. The surgeons
smile and tell us how well I'm healing but it doesn't
feel like it.

Happy

Time stopped when I was moved from intensive care. All day and night doctors and nurses cycle in and out of the room. They shine lights in my eyes, and then scribble on charts and hand me pills and ask if I've shit yet and tell me to drink more water. I glared at the TV while a nurse removed my catheter, tried to smile when she said "All done," but I was flushed with shame. It was excruciating, like a fishing lure tearing from my bladder, down my penis, and popping out of my dick hole.

I snag the eye patch and snap it over my right eye. During the operation my eyeballs rotated out, and now I look like a walleye. The double vision and nystagmus are so bad it makes me sick. The other day, I threw up all over myself and none of my visitors moved. Ma looked around when she walked in, exhaled like she was going to kill somebody, then wiped the gunk from my chin and stalked off to get a nurse.

A stuffed parrot is next to me in bed. Bouquets on the dresser. Get-well cards stand upright like cheery billboards. The U of Miami Medical School T-shirt Dad bought is draped over the chair with a Miami Hurricanes hat on top of it. The checkerboard Ma drew is on the bedside table; a nickel and two pennies sit on the squares.

After the toilet flushes, Ma tiptoes around the corner but hurries to my bed when she sees I'm awake. "Ali Baba! You're up! How you feeling? How's your tummy?"

"Shitty."

"You have a good nap?"

"Nope."

"What do you want to do?"

"Nothing."

"Well, too bad. You heard them!" She mimics the doctors, tells me I need to start doing as much as I can. She has nicknames for all of them and keeps asking for the chunk of brain tissue they excised. When Dr. Heros stands behind me, breathing on my sutured neck, reminding me not to touch the incision, Ma asks him if he brought us truffles.

"Let's go, let's go! You need to get going." She claps. "You eat that green Jell-O? Shit looked bad!"

"Ma, will you close the shades all the way? It's too bright. Jesus, you're being loud."

"Your first day of physical therapy is tomorrow," she says seriously. "So get ready. Let's get this party started!" she laughs, and closes the blinds. "That better?"

"Oh, great."

"What do you want to do now? We have a whole day! Come on, Ali!"

"Fucking nothing," I blurt. "Nothing, Ma. I'm tired and I hurt all over. I'm not having fun."

"Want to go rolling around the halls? We have to do something. Want to play checkers again?"

"I already beat you, Ma," I say, feebly lifting my arms. "I am the champ, and now, I retire. PEACE!" I shout. "Let me sleep."

"Ali, do I have to remind you? This is not a democracy." She stares at me. "You might think it is, but it's not. What are we going to do? *Now*. Right now."

She waits for my answer.

"Fine." I huff. "Let's get the fuck out of here. Shit."

In the hallway, Ma pushes me up from the wheelchair into the walker. The corridor starts spinning, faster and faster, and I have to sit back down.

"It's OK, Ali." She rubs my shoulders like a boxing trainer. "Take your time."

When I'm ready, I lean forward, and she pushes me up and then stands guard behind me. The world spins again but I don't go down because Ma's forearms press into my sides. She holds me up until my feet can gather under me, then guides me toward the walker and gently loosens her squeeze.

Even holding the walker, I have no balance. It feels like I'm on a tightrope in a cyclone. I lurch and lean and waver, and because I can't feel my face, I don't notice the snot running from my nose until I taste it. The walker slides out of my hands and falls to the floor, but Ma catches me as I go down.

"It looks like they shaved Batman's symbol in there," she says when I stand again. The cut goes from the top vertebrae of my spine, up my neck, to the bump on the back of my head. It's stapled shut, but it's leaking and I can't stop picking at it.

"Ma, it's really itchy. I'm gonna scratch the shit out of it."

"No." Her arms clamp around my midsection. "No. You are not, Al. Nope."

"Please?"

"No way, man! Don't even think about it."

My weight is totally on my legs, but when I lift my hands off of the walker the tiles rush toward my face. The hallway spins, and I start to fall, gasping, "Shit fuck shit," but her arms loop under my armpits. She lifts, steadying me until I can boost myself up with my shoulders.

"You're good," she says, straining. "Take your time."

"It feels like my brain is fuckin' pouring out of there." I lock my arms on the walker so my legs don't have to support me at all. "Does it look all right?"

"It's red and wet and pretty wicked, but it's fine." She pauses, and I think she's going to lecture me about scratching it, but she doesn't. "We'll take some pictures later. Gotta document it. It's a good look," she laughs, "but you got competition around here."

I'm on a hospital floor for patients with head trauma, so nearly each person we see has a scarred-up skull. Each day Ma has rolled me through the halls and we argue about whose haircut is best, Zipperhead, the old guy with staples arcing all over his head, or the pale woman who looks like a snow globe filled with lightning.

"They don't got shit on me, Ma."

She laughs, says, "I'm not sure, Tiny."

"You know I'm right, Ma."

"Ali, *come on*. You can tell me I'm right later. Listen to me now. Why don't you just use the walker? Don't try it all by yourself."

I settle my weight into my feet and try to stand. Sweat pours down my face. Beneath the eye patch my eye burns. When I look at my hands, everything spins out of control and I body-shudder. I stare ahead, gurgling and spitting into the hallway. There's no way I can do it. The vertigo gets worse when I just think about taking a step.

"Come on, Al. It'll happen. Just use the walker a little. That's what it's for."

"OK. OK. OK."

I shift all of my weight to my arms but keep my slippers on the floor so it looks like I'm standing. Shuffling my feet over the hospital tiles, I softly lift and swing the walker forward so it hops and looks like I'm taking steps.

"What's that, Al?"

"Walking with the walker."

"*What?* I don't think so, man."

"Using the walker to walk, Ma. *It's what it's for.*"

"Nope." She says it like she's struggling not to scold me. "You're cheating. Cheater, cheater."

"Walking." I swing myself forward, not using my legs at all. "I love walking!"

"Cheating." She fist-pinches my side and tells me to stop. "Use your legs and the walker. It's OK, Ali. Don't be a cheater."

"I was walking."

"No way. Use the walker, dude. You have to do it. If you don't use the walker, you're grounded."

"Come on, Ma!"

I groan when she starts singing "Your Cheating Heart." Other hall-shufflers are watching us and I'm fucking exhausted and embarrassed. "Let's go, Ali!" Ma shouts.

I start to tumble when the weight moves into my feet but her arms lock against me. Muscles spasm like animals trapped under my skin, but she's right there. I move the walker a few inches, listing and bellyaching, but with Ma's help, I use the walker and my halting legs and take my first step.

"Shit, Ma, I need to sit down. Right now."

For the rest of the day Ma pushes my wheelchair around the hospital. Back and forth through the sterile halls until I have the energy to try again. We ride the elevator. We peek into rooms. We roll through the cafeteria's hubbub, even spend a few minutes outside in the sunshine before returning to the head-trauma floor. In a couple of hours, I can make it a yard with the walker. By the end of the day, I'm almost a dozen feet down the hallway before I collapse into the wheelchair.

"I'm through," I say. I've barely gone anywhere. "Shit, Ma, I'm pooped."

"You done good, Ali." She whistles, wheeling me back to my room. "Real good. You da man!"

The hospital sounds bizarre as we roll down the hall: dozens of TVs playing different shows, shouts and pained moans and clicking carts and rickety wheelchairs and the knell of medical machinery. The strange orchestra washes over us until we're back in the silence of my room. It's a scorched black except for a machine's blinking next to my bed.

"Ma . . . Can we go again tomorrow?"

"Sure, Al. It'll be fun. And you should always listen to your Ma."

"That was pretty awesome, huh?" I'm dog-tired and grinning. "Aren't you glad I spent so much time in the gym instead of doing my chores?" I'm still smiling when she flips the lights on. "Decided to do all that lifting instead of digging up stumps in the garden? I know you're going to start pumping iron now. Get all big, aren't you, Ma? Oh yeeeaaaaah!!!" I elongate the word and laugh, but it sounds like a balloon squeaking out air.

"*Shhhheeeeeeeeiiiiiit!*" she grumbles, but I can tell she's ecstatic. I'm out of my bed, trying to walk. I've never seen her smile wider. "Ali. That, what you just said, is some bullshit," she says, helping me onto the mattress. She leans down to kiss me, says, "But if it makes you feel better to think that way, be my guest."

4

Seagulls were arguing outside the dark window when I woke. The sliver of black sky between the curtains went bruised and then gleamed blue. When I looked away from the morning light, Ma was standing in the room, watching me. She gave me a kiss, then opened the blinds; she closed them again when I said that it was too much. Within minutes, the doctors came in and I squeezed fingers, opened my jaw like a snake, and slowly rotated my head. I took the eye patch off and tried to track their penlights. After looking at the gluey cut, they smiled, patted my sheet-bound foot, and then left. A second later, Ma said she needed to go for a stroll and walked out. I could hear them talking outside.

For hours, I've been playing a ruleless game of checkers against myself. I slide whelks and augers across the board, jump a flat black stone with a sand dollar. Bits of the beach trickle out of each shell, pouring over the Formica table and my sheets. The room smells brackish but it's better than the hospital's usual bleak stink.

There's a knock—the doctors must be back; they're the only ones who *clack-clack-clack* before whisking in to maneuver me around.

I say, "Come in." but for a few minutes, no one appears. "Fine, asshole." I mutter, hoping the wrong-door tapper hears me.

"May I join you?"

When the man looks around the corner, the first thing I notice is his priestly collar. He stands at the foot of my bed with a mottled Bible against his chest, smiling earnestly.

"Umm. I guess." I try to sit up. "Sure, come in."

"I hope you're having a pleasant day."

"It's OK, I think."

"Would it be all right if I prayed with you?" He has sun-plowed, leathery skin; it's impossible to guess his age. Trying to keep him in focus makes my head hurt worse. I want to laugh, tell him to hit the fucking road, but I can't speak. Saliva crackles in my mouth. I squint at him while he waits. My eyes bounce and the room sifts.

"I suppose. I mean, sure." I'm confused, sad with this stranger in my room.

"Would you prefer Spanish or English?" His accented words lilt tautly in the hospital air, and he hands me both versions of "The Lord's Prayer."

I start to weep when the room fills with Spanish. I make wet mashing sounds like I'm trying to pray but end up smacking *shitshitshit* while he intones. Eyes closed, he holds my hands. I start to shake and stare out at the crease of blue sky, but I'm not there. I'm in the bodega again, the soft flow of bodies buoying me around, burning the tarnish away.

And then there's nothing. In the lancing quiet, he says, "Thank you."

When I look back from the window the man is gone, but his voice is still fluttering mothlike through the room. There's a knock next door. The man, faint and sincere and asking. One of his pamphlets sits on my shells.

I've never been a believer. I couldn't even hear him pray over the backwash of voices in my head, but I didn't want the priest to go. I need to tell someone that I'd wanted to be the body next to me in intensive care. I wished to be the boy who didn't make it. And I need to tell someone that, in that same instant, the boy's family bawling as he died, I was so happy that he hadn't made it. That the tangible darkness in the ICU had turned away from my bed. That *he* had drifted into the bottomless black. That it wasn't me.

5

THE AIRPORT DAZZLES AROUND US. A YAWNING GROVE OF glass and light and intolerable noise, it makes me sick. A teenager stops unwinding his Cinnabon when the man pushing my wheelchair says, "'Scuze us." The kid steps out of the way, deliberately slow, and then stares and chews. The eye patch feels like it's been tattooed to my face. A woman leaning against a potted palm watches me and then speaks to the man next to her behind a cupped hand. I finger-stretch the hospital bracelet. After the security check, a little girl points until her arm is snatched down. A man yanks her away.

Ma walks beside me, pressing my shoulder like it's a brake. But I'm just luggage. My head whips about with each bump.

"Fucking shit." I drool. "Come on, man. What the fuck?"

"Could we slow down? Please?" Ma says it the same way she used to tell me I was grounded, tired but not bullshitting: *That's three weeks, Al. Keep talking and we'll start adding days. OK, then. One month.* "Stop for a second." Her hand is a brick against my chest. "We have to go slower. He had *brain surgery.*" She says it like the guy didn't hear it the other ten times she told him, like she would seethe *you fucking ass-hole.*

When the airline grunt leaned down to introduce himself, I thought some asshole from the Make-a-Wish Foundation had sent Captain Kangaroo to see me. He held his pants up with one hand and wiped his nose with the other. Eyes twitching, just inches from my face, he shouted like he thought I was deaf or retarded.

"Sure," Captain Cocaine says to Ma huffily, jerking the wheelchair to a stop. "Just trying to get you there. You know, make sure you catch your flight and every-thing." I start to roll forward, slowly, with Ma's hand clamped on my shoulder. In seconds, we're going faster than we were before. Everyone in the airport stares at us.

The incision is covered with fresh bandages for the trip home, but it must be bleeding through. I run my fingers under the dressing and find nuggets of caked pus. When I reach behind me, I pretend my hands are birds circling above a smoldering field, swooping in for the kill, plucking tiny animals off and then vanishing into the flawlessly blue sky.

I flick the scabby crumbs at strangers' food and cups.

HAPPY

The guy wheels me to the gate, turns the chair so I'm facing the rows of seated and gaping people, and then leaves without saying a word. People try not to look at me and I turn red. Ma kisses my forehead, then picks the bloody seeds out of my hair and kneads my shoulders. She gently runs her fingertips against the side of my head like she's trying to scrape some of what I'm feeling away.

The days, which had seemed painstakingly deliberate when I was in the hospital, have turned into a line of burning gunpowder. "Congratulations. It's time to start outpatient care," the doctors shouted as they filled out my release forms. "You get to go home!" the nurses chirped, hugging me. "You're going to be great!" they said. But I wanted to stay. I think I'm leaving because the insurance company won't cover more hospital days. This afternoon, after the good-byes, Ma wheeled me out of the hospital into the boiling day. It's been less than two weeks since I had surgery.

I listen to passengers talk about what's wrong with me while Ma and a stewardess help me into a window seat. I feel lame and terrible. I'm sensitive to light and the smallest sounds are tympanic. I pull the blind down and close my unpatched eye. Ma packs airline pillows behind me so my head doesn't flop. She and the stewardess tuck blankets and more pillows so I'm motionless. I feel like I'm made out of glass.

The pillows fall away and my head slumps when the airplane backs from the gate. My skull smacks against the window shade as the engines roar. Ma says "Fuck it" as the jet streaks down the runway. Unclicking her seat belt as we rise into the sky, she rearranges the pillows. The stewardess tells her that she needs to sit down, but Ma ignores her. The plane lifts and drops and lifts while she works. It swoops and dips, and then finally, after a long, curving climb, it straightens out.

"How you doing?" Ma exhales, patting my thigh when she's done. "Al?"

We hit more turbulence and the metal wings flap like a bird's.

"Not so hot. I'm going to use one of those bags." I resnap the eye patch in place and give her a look that says I don't want to talk. Not for a long time.

"Let me know what you need," she says, eyes filling with tears. "I'm really trying to make this better for you. Ali, I'm trying."

I turn away from her and press my head into the quaking cabin wall.

X

1

November 1999, St. Paul

FOR ALMOST TWO MONTHS, I'VE BEEN SITTING IN A WHEEL-chair, naming what I can hardly see. The wheelchair is *honeybucket* and *halo of knives with eye patch*. The front porch is *city of no faces*, and then, after a few weeks, *the smell of cooking meat. Sucklife* and *emptied chest*, the morning birds sing to me, *hushhushhush*. By noon they're just ghosts of music.

Everything outside the glassed-in porch comes to me like I'm the boy in the bubble, but I love the sunlight red-shifting over my closed eyes. The mail carrier whistles down Osceola and I drag myself inside and fall on the living room floor. In the back of the house, Ma sings over NPR, tooling away on her sculptures. Letters drop through the slot, the whistling winnows away, and I use my walker to gimp back to the porch. I ignore the envelopes, the cards that come each day. The wind bows the warm glass, and I hear my college friends working toward graduation—Macalester College, my college, is just four blocks away. I crane with the eye patch off and sweat beads my cheeks. With my hand pressed against the glass, I can feel the ebb of campus in my fingertips.

Not being able to read is making me crazy. Words crawl across the page like they're alive, like bugs. They jump. They tick. So I barely open my eyes. Everything feels right there in front of me, but it's all out of reach. It's all a tease. It would be easier if I were blind.

I've always had nicknames, and in my head, I kill each one of them. But sitting in the wheelchair, I can control nothing—and I'm forced to watch them rise from the earth like zombies. I cannot look away from my thoughts. I want to move, to lose myself in a book, to get better—but I can't.

I imagine myself lounging on the lawn in front of Old Main, laughing with my friends, watching the night sky. In my head, I go to all my classes. I take my baseball hat off and raise my hand; I ask questions and know every answer. In my head, I can read again and pore over each assigned essay. Foucault and Baldwin, Kimiko Hahn and John Ashbery, Marcus Garvey, Agamben, Joyce and Beckett—I can't get enough homework. I would do anything to write a paper.

The mail truck is toddling by when I look, but my eyes don't work right anymore—there are two white-blue blocks of malignant light. My stomach sours as they bounce down the street.

I imagine I'm building a raku kiln outside of the ceramic studio when I close my eyes again. Dropping orange-hot vessels into garbage cans of paper, leaves, cardboard, and pine needles. Oxidizing. Reduction. Glazes crackling, the world around me all smoke and flame. I picture myself setting the Dumpster on fire with smoldering sawdust after the firing, and because my legs work again, I sprint to the faucet inside. Back and forth, back and forth—but the fire won't go out. The sculpture professor stands at the door with his hands on his hips, watching me try to put the blaze out with tiny cups of water. He tips back his cowboy hat and shakes his head, then walks slowly into the art department. When he returns, he drops a hose over my tennis shoes and walks away.

I laugh out loud, coughing into the porch's opened-coffin light, and Ma rushes through the house.

"You OK, Ali?" she asks. "What's going on out here?"

With my eyes still closed, I flop my head back and tell her that I'm fine. "Mail just came," I say. "Think I'm going to take a nap."

She touches my shoulder. As she sways, my eyelids darken, go pink, and then darken again. "Let me know if you want anything," she says, sorting through the mail. She stacks my letters with the unopened others. She waits for me to speak, standing behind me for a few minutes, before returning to her studio.

My eyelids go white when I face west.

In my head, I watch a bump of porcelain clay spin deliriously on the potter's wheel. I squeeze a wet sponge over it, and water droplets arrow from the circling mound. There is music coming from the clay-speckled stereo: the Beatles, the first CD Ma bought me. *Woke up, got out of bed . . .* The black speakers are daubed, fingerprinted, with silt. I press my hands together and the rotating mound of clay grows into a spike. The body, my body, stays at the potter's wheel, but I can see myself splitting away and walking right through the studio's glass wall. Campus is alive today. Everyone is lingering outside and the lilacs are in bloom. The full bushes sweetheavy and bright. Friends stand outside the library and yell, *ALEX! So good to see you!* and I walk to them with my working legs. *How are you, man?* they ask, and I tell them that I'm tired, that I'm not sleeping so well. I say, *Shit, things are pretty good.* But my smile is fake and heavy. *No, wait,* I shout as they start to walk away from me, *that is a lie. I'm a liar. Things are not good. Things are not good at all.*

When the phone rings I'm so startled I fall out of the wheelchair. The windows vibrate and the phone rings and rings and rings but I do not move. I close my eyes again. Running from the back of the house, Ma smacks the walls and yells, "Phonephonephone!"

"No!" I yell over my shoulder. "Don't get it!"

"You sure, Ali?"

"Positive. Just stop answering it. No more."

"Hello?" she says sweetly after picking it up. "Yes?"

She tells whomever it is that I'm not feeling well again today. "He appreciates it, Casey," she says. "He really does. It'll make him feel better just knowing you called." She asks him to call again soon, to swing by some time, before hanging up.

"Casey and Dan and Lars today. Erin called yesterday," she says, walking onto the porch. "I know you don't want to, Al, but you should call them back."

"No."

"You need to call them back." She bounces a hand on my shoulder.

"No, I don't." I try to slough it off. "I don't want to see anyone."

"Al."

"Ma."

"Oh, Al." She sighs, giving up. "Can I get you anything? Do you want some more water?"

"Nope." I push play on the boom box Ma set next to me and *In Their Own Voices* plays. W. S. Merwin recites "The River of Bees" and I clear my throat in the dusty sunlight. *Men think they are better than grass.* I turn up the volume and exhale to let Ma know that she can go.

Ten minutes after leaving, she returns and sets a glass on the ledge and sits on the floor. The autumn light closes fast now that winter's coming, and soon I'm sipping water in the dark. Ma breathes behind me and we listen.

"Glad you like the CDs," she says, standing after it

clicks off. "I'll get more for you tomorrow." In the dark, insects plink the porch bulb above us. It's staggeringly bright when she turns it on.

"Leave it off, Ma. OFF!"

"You want a snack?" she asks, ignoring my assholishness. "A little somethin' something to get you to dinner?"

"Nope."

She flips the switch so I'm sitting in the dark and walks into the house. I used to love listening to baseball games on the radio, but I can't stand it now. Hearing the crack of the bat and applause and play-by-play makes me weep, so I put in the next poetry CD and push play. Like fireflies, homes down the street start bursting to light.

I'd begged Ma to find a rental near Mac, told her that daily visits from my friends would help me heal. But I don't want to see anyone now—not like this—not while I'm in this body. I don't keep my eyes open much because of the double vision and nystagmus, and I can hardly walk. I'm in bed or in the wheelchair on the porch all day. I only leave when Ma says it's time for physical therapy. If she didn't make me go, I wouldn't move. I can't do anything I want to do. This is not my body. I'm a cripple.

The dark seconds dawdle toward sunup while I toss in the new bed Ma bought for me. I do not sleep anymore; I feel like I'm covered in centipedes. All night I reach in and out of memories, but as the neighbor's bedroom light flicks on in the morning, I'm left with the same one. The first bed I remember Ma making for me was egg foam and a slat of cardboard, raised off of the floor by bricks. She'd sewn a heart-shaped blanket and a life-sized man in suspenders for me. One night, looking under my bed for toys, my hand curled around a furred lump. No matter how I squeezed the frozen thing or pushed it around with my toy cars, I could not bring the dead mouse back to life.

From my new bed I watch the darkness, as again and again surgeons take everything but anger out of my skull. In the dark, it pulses, gloms like a trophy on the bookshelf. A fetus in a jar. I gaze at the ceiling, thinking about all the things I miss and hate. My new body. My girlfriend. My friends. My life. And I'm too afraid to let anyone see me. I've always been afraid people would think I was a pussy, and now, that's exactly what I am.

Yarrow was the only person I wanted to see at first. She picked us up at the airport and stopped by the house a lot the first weeks. When she slept over we lay in my new bed—barely talking, touching slowly. Dizzy with vertigo. I tried to remember her press and contour but it was empty. I've started feeling more alone when she's in the room with me. It's like my insides have been unplugged, scrambled. I can tell she's having a hard time seeing me this way. The last month she was so busy with school and cross-country, she didn't come around much. I want someone close to me, but it reminds me of how frail I am. Sitting in the wheelchair with Yarrow next to me, I am vulnerable and panicky. And now, tension fills the house when she visits.

After Yarrow left yesterday morning, Ma said she didn't think my girlfriend should sleep over. I stared at her, hard. I just need the warmth of a body next to me in bed, I wanted to tell Ma, but I was so angry the words gagged me.

"Tough shit!" I stammered.

"You should ask her to take care of you then!" Ma's face twisted as she yelled. "Do you think she'll really do everything for you? Do you really? That's bullshit! I'll just get out of here. Adios! She can take care of you!"

I slammed my door, curled onto the floor, and wept.

2

"TIME TO GO, AL," MA SHOUTS, SCRAMBLING THROUGH THE house. "We're late!"

Above Osceola, the sky is curdled with clouds. Each time a leaf falls the neighborhood trees stretch skinnier, prehistoric. After doing my therapy exercises I haven't moved from the wheelchair. I've been on the porch and Ma's stayed in her studio all day. We've been talking less and less.

She runs in and picks up my glass of cranberry juice and sings. "Gotta mooooove, man!"

"Already?" I exhale. "Fuck."

"You're getting better, Al. You are." She picks my eye patch up off the floor, helps me out of the chair, makes sure I'm holding on to the door handle, and then lugs the wheelchair down to the sidewalk. She guides me down the steps and into the chair, and then sets the walker in front of me. It's a twenty-foot marathon to the car door.

She claps, says, "Way to go, Ali," then kisses me after I make it.

"I'm so sick of this shit." I bow over the walker, then slump in the car.

I STARE HUNGRILY AT THE OTHER PATIENTS WHILE I WAIT for my physical therapy appointment. All of the bodies being maneuvered around like fucked-up chess pieces. But these groaning minutes at the rehabilitation clinic have become the best part of my day: in the garish light, being surrounded by the broken and dying is a gift. I feel good. I feel myself get stronger by watching their misery, smiling to myself each time the goateed guy in leg and neck braces collapses, or, even better yet, the morning I realized the old lady with the IV and gray Afro wasn't being wheeled in anymore.

And when the rehab therapist says, "Hello, Alex!" I forget about everyone else. She grins—I'm younger than everyone else who comes to rehab. I'm still strong enough to get better.

Hooked to her waist by a strap that won't let me fall, I drag myself between the balance beams. I groan and sweat and shuffle crookedly with the walker until my body trembles. I totter around like I'm on a leash. My body quivers when she has me stand without any help. "Up straight, up straight," she says as I lean. The tether cinches tight and she catches me when I fall. I make it fifteen seconds without reaching out, and then thirty. One minute. Two.

When I sit, my body shakes uncontrollably.

"Yes!" She nods. "Good work, Alex! You want to try sitting on the ball again?"

"I'm pretty tired." I grin at her. "I think that's all I got."

"OK. We'll do it next time. Do you go to speech therapy today?"

"Nope. I'm done. Went a few weeks ago. I. Need. To. Enunciate. And. Slow. Down." I laugh. "But I don't have to go back."

"Great. Next time we'll get you standing on a piece of foam. You should start trying that at home."

"Sounds good." I say it tiredly, but I mean it. I will do whatever it takes to get better. I've made progress each of my appointments, and at home, I do my exercises until I'm exhausted.

"Yeah?"

"Sure."

When she gets back from the office, I'm still sweating and she hands me three sheets of paper— each of the xeroxes has a picture of a man performing simple balance exercises with text beneath it that explains the technique. Standing on one leg. Raising the knee in front of the body. Lifting a leg to one side.

"Excellent job today," she says as I flip through the pages. "Alex, you're doing so well. I think, along with your exercises, you should start using a cane. What do you think? What color do you want?"

It's a warm afternoon so Ma ignores my protests, says we're going to go for a walk, and parks along River Road. On the running path, she crunches my wheelchair through fallen leaves. Pushing me, she whistles and sings. Light waterfalls over my closed eyes.

Ma's leaning in front of me when I wake up. "Maple," she says, handing me a red leaf. "Same color as your cane! It's a sign! Good things are happening!"

"Sure," I yawn. "Whatever."

When the wheelchair slams over a crack, she clutches my shoulder so I don't fall out of the chair. She says, "Oh shit, sorry, Ali!"

"Fuckin' A." I grumble. "Fuuuck. Come on!"

The muscles in my neck are still weak and the steroids are making me fat. I feel like a baby being taken out for a stroll. We roll on in silence, and each bump reminds me of how much I need her help.

"What did they have you do today, Ali?"

"Same shit."

I'm stopped and turned; the wheelchair faces River Road. Across the street, cut tree limbs are piled on a lawn. Trash is mounded in the driveways of the million-dollar homes.

"Tomorrow's garbage day! Oooooooh, and some of those ones look good," she says, pointing at the sticks. "I need some of those, don't you think?"

"Ma, we got enough shit." Each time she says she's going to the supermarket she comes back with bags of clothes and boxes of knickknacks from the Goodwill and Salvation Army or other Twin Cities thrift stores. "You don't need them."

"For the art, Ali, for the art!"

"I'm getting cold, Ma. Can we go?"

"So what did you do today?" she asks again, circling me around, carefully this time.

"Told you. Standing and walking." I scrunch down as two joggers from my college swish by. "Same stuff I always do."

"You excited about the cane? Want to practice when we get home?"

"Probably not. I don't know. Maybe."

"Well, I got you some CD books from the library. You can check those out if you want. I'm going to make a store run, you need anything?"

"Hmmm. How 'bout a couple of Whoppers and some licorice? And I want one of those physio ball things."

"Sure you don't want White Castle?" she laughs. She knows the steroids make me feel like I'm starving. I've already put on twenty-five pounds. I'm moon-faced. "How 'bout a gunnysack of fish sandwiches? Teasing. Whatever you need, Ali. Whatever you need to feel better."

WITH THE SHOWER WATER JUDDERING DOWN ON ME, THE slamming door sounds like tentative thunder. "Al! Get out of there. Surprise, surprise!" Ma yells. The house rasps with footsteps. "Soooooooprrrriiiiiiiiissse!"

She knocks on the bathroom door. "You hear me, Ali?"

"Yeah, Ma." I lean into the wall to make sure I don't fall. While one hand lathers my face with soap, the other clings to the windowsill through the shower curtain. I will not let her bathe me. "Almost done. Be out soon."

I stand at the back of the tub, out of the spray, and practice my eye exercises. The water's white noise helps me focus and I track my finger back and forth with each eye, one at a time, and then do it a third time with both eyes open. They're starting to realign, but there are times when the double vision and vertigo make me dizzy and nauseous. My fingertip goes back and forth in front of me, Ma is running around the house, the water is like a thousand fingers tapping my body, and the next thing I know, I'm falling forward. My face smashes into the white metal.

"You OK, Al? Hey, Al, you OK?" Ma pounds the door, rattling the locked knob.

"Fine," I garble, pushing up to my hands and knees. Gloves of bloody water fall from my face. "Just slipped a bit."

"You OK? Did you fall?"

"Caught myself, Ma. Be out in a second." I lie flat in the tub until my nose stops bleeding. My ribs hurt.

When I shut the shower off twenty minutes later, she's breathing outside.

Happy

"Ma!" I yell, and sit on the toilet. I pee like a girl, towel off, and pull on a T-shirt. She's still there. "You can leave now!" I shimmy into my boxers and listen to her walk away, then grab the walker and stand. On the way to the kitchen, I clank past a sofa-sized stack of branches and cans of spray paint.

Ma's sitting at the table, whittling. A stick is bent, tied into a parabola in front of her. She doesn't say a word, just nods at the 50% MORE pack of Twizzlers and the Whoppers and fries on my plate.

That night, I lie in bed with my door closed, listening to the books on CD Ma got at the library. I pause and repeat words under my breath. Firming my lips and pointing my tongue, I try to enunciate clearly but my voice sounds like it's coming from a caved-in mine. Like I have shit in my mouth. Halfway through a Walter Mosley novel, I have to restart it because I have no idea what's going on. I listen to the first CD in the book again and then turn it off. It's pointless; my brain is mush.

Over Ma's radio, I hear her tools. She snaps sticks and sings for hours. She sleeps less than I do.

In the quiet, Ma locks the front door and then walks back through the house, shutting off the lights. I can hear her breathing when she stops to listen at my bedroom door.

3

I'VE BEEN SITTING AT MY COMPUTER, TRYING TO WRITE
e-mails all morning, but the voice recognition software
Ma got me doesn't work. I say, "Yo, Keenan, I'm not
doing shit, what are you up to?" and then squint at the
humongous font the program types. The text reads,
"Ho Kleenex! Um rot spooring tights,,,,,, clap are you
up two?" I speak slower and try again. "Yo yo Ma, I'm
sitting here in my room. You'll read this at the library.
Just wanted to say hi." The giant letters lumber across
the monitor. "Pogo spa, I'm splitting hearing tomb.
Yule read this at the lie berry. Just wanted Tuesday hi."

"Fuck you, machine," I say, kicking the desk and
wall before standing. There's laughter—two voices in
the living room—so, using the cane, I lurch out.

Ma and my friend Erin are sitting on the futon; they
look up when I tap around the corner.

"Erin's come to see you, Al!" Ma says, smiling

tightly. She knows I don't want to see anyone, but the look says I better not say shit.

"Hi, Al!" Erin hugs me. "How are you?"

I'm not sure what to do now that the house's quiet has been broken. I've been telling Ma I didn't want my friends to visit, and I'm shocked Erin's here. I've known her since my freshman year, but we've never been very close.

"You look great, Al," she says. "Nice to finally see you."

"Yeah, wow." I say quietly. I'm so embarrassed to be seen. "Thanks for coming over."

"Nice talking to you, Erin." Ma says, "but if you'll excuse me, I need to go work on some art!" She tells me that some of the guys are going to visit later and then walks back to her studio and turns the stereo on.

Erin and I lie on the living room floor. I can feel her looking at me.

"So, Al, how are you doing?"

"Yeah, I'm fine, I suppose." The ceiling looks like a rain-strafed parking lot. "I mean, this all kind of sucks." I laugh sourly.

"I'm sure. So what's going on?" she asks softly. "What's it like?"

I don't know where to start. I don't know anymore. "It's all different than it used to be." I sip a water bottle and smile. "Man, that sounds stupid, doesn't it? It's really fine. I'm just tired a lot. I can't see shit."

"No, it doesn't." She quiets and waits for me to go on.

"It's like everything is moving all the time. Like I'm

looking through drizzle or something. Striated. No, that's not it. I don't know. Shit."

Erin reaches over and holds my hand, and I don't want to pull away. It feels good. "What do you mean, Al?"

"When I look, everything is jumping and spinning. Things change size. I feel like I'm going to fall all the time."

"Oh, Al, I'm so sorry."

"It's OK, really. It's like Al in Wonderland," I laugh, and after a moment, she smiles and laughs too.

For an hour Erin listens to me try to describe my twirling world. I tell her about rehab, the exercises I do each day, and she acts fascinated. She wants to know more, and for a few minutes while I talk, we prop up against the couch and stare at the empty street, and nothing seems wrong.

4

Ma tells my friends to take me to the Mac football
game that Saturday, and she swaddles me in so many
jackets it feels like I'm wearing an inflatable sumo suit.
On campus, I have to sit in the wheelchair so I don't
get too tired, but Lars and Kirkman love it. While we
wait for Christian and Casey, they push me around the
dorm courtyard, popping wheelies and making race-
car noises, turning so sharply that I tilt up on one
wheel and claw at the armrests.

When I ask Lars for a smoke, he presses it into my
lips like he's throwing a dart. "Motlow! Motlow!" he
shouts, jacking his fists into the air above his head.
"Good to have you back! Great to see you, my man."
He fist-trumpets and says he missed me, that the eye
patch is *badass*.

"Don't be jealous, ol' buddy." My words scatter in
the cold air. "Wait 'til the pirate jokes start." The ciga-

261

rette tastes like shit, but the sooner I get back to my old life, the sooner everything will be fine.

"The guys say hi," Kirkman says about my teammates.

I say, "That's nice," and smile, but tell him that I don't want to come watch practice.

The four of them walk quietly behind me, and my wheelchair croaks down the sidewalk. Our breath expands in the freezing air. Someone keeps clapping their gloved hands.

We're almost to the stadium, the air fragile with our silence, when Christian laughs and asks where I've been hiding out.

"Live right down there." I hitchhike my thumb up at the Osceola street sign as we roll by it. "Landlord is a fucking piano tuner. So which one of you assholes is going to start taking me to my rehab appointments?" I laugh.

The cigarette lops from Lars's mouth, and he raises both hands sheepishly. A wreath of smoke haloes his head.

"If you twist my arm, I just might skip some classes," Casey sniggers. "But you gotta pay me. Pay the piper."

"Yeah?"

"You got it," Casey says.

"Name the time, Motlow. I'll take you."

At the top of the stadium ramp, friends circle around my wheelchair, asking me what I've been up to. I say that I haven't been doing much of anything and they quiet and shuffle from side to side, rubbing their hands.

"Me and Ma," I laugh. "Cold chilling. Nothing like being twenty-one and kicking it all day with your Ma, right? *Shiiiiiitty!*"

Sitting in the wheelchair, eating the popcorn Karen gave me when we passed the concession stand, I watch my friends try to find seats. They have to ask some parents in the front row to move because my wheelchair won't fit up the steps. They point at me. Humiliated, I give them all a little wave, and the parents fold up their blankets and climb the bleachers. The guys come back laughing; someone says they should take me everywhere.

"We could use you to pick up chicks, Happy!"

"FUCK YOU!" I laugh, but it kinks up my insides. This is why I didn't want to go out. Rows of football players are doing jumping jacks and I think about how each of them will crash into each other all afternoon, and I will get tired just clapping. None of my friends understand this.

At the end of the first quarter the Fighting Scots are getting killed, but other than the coaches and players and a smattering of parents, no one cares. Everyone is laughing, hardly watching the game, and joking about how sick they are of getting asked about their post-graduation plans. There's still another semester to go, but the seniors are already checked out. They wave invisible diplomas. Toss imaginary mortarboards into the sky.

My wheelchair crowds their legs and they talk about how much fun Halloween was this year. "You should have come, Happy." Someone laughs. "Eye patch and shit, you're already a pirate. Arrrggghhh!"

I fake-laugh, mouth *"What the fuck did I tell you?"* to Lars.

He takes a sip from the flask he's hiding in his vest and shrugs. "You're fucking crazy, Motlow. Fuck 'em."

We return from the parking lot after halftime a few minutes into the third quarter. My friends have been getting fucked up, and they laugh at the scoreboard, dancing ridiculously and singing the Gigolo. Casey rides in my lap as we roll in front of the packed stands and it's dreadful. Everyone turns and watches me.

5

It doesn't matter that I Zorro the cane through the air at the passing cars: they won't stop for me. For me, the fucking crippled guy standing in the crosswalk. The guy wearing an eye patch, shouting cusses, and waving a red cane.

The last week I've been walking home from the dorms each day after rehab. It might take forever, but I can do it by myself now. Since the football game two weeks ago, Casey or Lars has taken me to the clinic, and after my appointment, I tell them that I don't want to go home. I want to hang out. So they take me back to campus. I call Ma to tell her that she doesn't need to get me, that I need my workout, and then stay in the dorms all day. I have a few drinks or smoke and chew. I leave whenever I want.

Like the sun's been painted over, the day goes black as I wait at the edge of the street. Light snow falls through the after-work headlights.

"Hey, fuckers!" Leaning against a parked Volvo, I yell at the cars, jabbing the cane like an old man. "Hello, all of you lousy assholes. Can you see me?" During a break in traffic, I gimp into Snelling, but a quarter of the way to the other side, I slow and limp and drag the cane. With cars lined up on each side of me the crosswalk becomes a blinding hallway.

As I clip by the church parking lot, a black car pulls beside me, but it's gotten too dark for me to clearly see anything. The car stereo is thumping, ominous. Snow trembles through its bluewhite headlights. I don't look, but I know the black car is pacing my tottering walk.

When I near the block's end, it's completely dark. I stop to catch my breath and the car is still there, engine purring.

The stereo turns off. The passenger window eases down. My heart coils and turns in my chest. If I run, I'll fall. I've worked too hard to get jumped. The last thing I need right now is to freeze frostbitten or dead after getting my ass kicked.

"Hey, guy!" A voice lows from the car. "Hold up a sec. Guy!"

I focus on my slipping Adidas and keep stumbling. The cane punches holes in the new snow. My hands are frozen, but I'm drenched with sweat under my jacket. Steam rises from my arms.

I have never not wanted to fight before, but slipping through the wintery slop, I'm afraid. I'm just starting to figure out this new body. There's no way I can start over again.

"Hey, guy! Stop a minute. I got to ask you a question."

"I'm late, sorry I can't help you." I hum softly and squeeze the cane grip. At the corner, the car speeds up and turns right, locking up the brakes, stopping against the curb, blocking my path.

"Listen here, fuckface!" the voice shouts. "I got a question for you! So come here, motherfucker! I got to ask you something!"

It's so dark I can't see more than three feet in front of me. I can't see anything. My eyelashes are thick with snow, and over the other eye, the eye patch feels like an ice puck. I'm trembling. I can't move.

"Motherfucker!" the voice yells. "I said, I have a question for you!"

"Man, I don't want any trouble. Please? I'm all fucked up already." Without looking up from the snowy sidewalk, I raise the cane in front of me. "See?"

"Oh no you don't, motherfucker!" the voice howls, but then it changes pitch. "You muthafucka, I got a question for you!" I know exactly who it is, and when I look up, the dome light turns on. Casey's smiling in the starkly lit car. "*I'm all fucked up already,*" he laughs, then says, "Fuck, man, I saw you walking and wanted to know if you needed a lift. I was just fucking with you, Al."

"Fuck you, Case. You fucking asshole. You scared the shit out of me." My heart is pounding.

"Sorry," he laughs. "It's too easy—but shit, man, you should have seen your face! Anyway, you want a ride or what? I got to get rolling."

"Thanks, man. I'm good."

"You sure? It's cold as balls out."

"Yep. I got to do this, man. Got to."

"Veddy good den, friend," he says in a terrible Indian accent. "I go go now! Veddy veddy good!"

After Casey drives away, I lumber on, stopping at the end of each block, exhausted but filling with weary elation. Snow sprinkles over me as I weave and stutter-step. For five blocks, I get to be in a solitude of my own choosing. No one is watching over me, telling me what I need to do to get better, saying that I can do it. No one is asking if I need anything. I have a bottle of gin and a baggie of pot in my jacket. The next party I go to at Mac I'm going to score some blow and shrooms. I was supposed to be home hours ago but I'm walking there by myself, and right now, this is exactly what I need.

Cigarette smoke somersaults through the falling snow as I stand, concentrating on the lit house windows like they're wavering video screens.

In a home on Goodrich a man looks down, mouth pulled wide, singing and towel-drying wineglasses. He swings the delicate bulbs through the air and dances from room to room after turning on all the lights.

In a kitchen on Sargent, a woman points a hand and jaws to an invisible person, a paring knife in her other hand. When she stops talking, she hunches over. Her cheeks tighten as she focuses and starts to cut.

I think about how my skin opened like a hungry red mouth when I cut into my wrist that night in Portland.

The way Julie's eyes turned fragile—changing colors—
when she saw what I'd done. Snow switchbacks to the
ground softly and I think about how good it has always
felt to hurt myself. The neighborhood is fragmented,
milky orange and diamondy, and the nothingness
inside me seems impossibly heavy. I only know how to
return all of the love people give me with cruelty. Cars
and trucks and semis fluster through the dark a block
away on Snelling Avenue. Doors close and a car alarm
meeps. Kids shout happily in the falling white. It
sounds like I'm inside a music box, and eyes closed,
listening to it all. I think about how I've always been
trying to cleave something from me. But now, it feels
like there's nothing left to cut away, or maybe none of
it matters anyway. It's never mattered. There's *just
this*.

The snow turns icy and I lie down on the sidewalk.
I'm not going to return to Mac this year. My friends
will graduate and move away and next year, I'll be a
fucking *super senior*. I will stumble through campus,
catatonic or talking maniacally to myself, putting anything inside me to get myself to stop thinking about
this. But for the first time since I woke up and was
alive, somehow, all of my brokenness—cuts and tears
and gashed memory—feels like it might be mending.

The wind uproars through the bald trees. Dervish-
ing through the streetlight, the snowflakes are a copper
horde of butterflies. They vanish on the wet black concrete.

Banging the front door behind me, I blunder around

the house, out of breath and pinging and clanging the cane until, in the back of the house, Ma turns off her radio.

"Yo, Ma!" I yell, tossing my coat on the floor. "What are we having for dinner? MAAAA!"

Ma walks into the kitchen wordlessly. She uncovers the food she's cooked, stares hard at the clock, then says she already ate.

"Casey wanted me to say what's up to you." I sit and laugh. "He's going to take me to PT again tomorrow. Cool?"

The burner burps to blue flame, and Ma drops a black skillet on the stove.

"Ma! Yo yo Ma!" I get up and Godzilla-hug her from side to side, trying to get her to smile. She doesn't even squirm away. "It's beautiful out there! You check it out? Ma, it's gorgeous!"

"You're late." Her voice is threadbare. She sets a mug of tea and a plate on the table, then asks how my day was but interrupts my answer to ask why she smells smoke and booze.

"My friends are so much fun." I squeeze the mug's warmth. I tell her that I need be around them now, and sometimes, whether I like it or not, *they* like to party. She frowns. "They don't listen to me, Ma, and they make me feel so good. You know? Starting to feel like I can do this shit!"

"You can, Ali." She smiles vacantly. "You are doing it."

She forks a pork chop onto my plate and scoops me some rice. Next to the bowl of salad, she balances the

Mickey Mouse spoon on top of the jar of homemade dressing.

"That's really nice," she says, briskly walking out. The stereo in her studio shuts off. Ten silent minutes later, she returns to the kitchen and sits across from me.

"But tomorrow night," she says, starting to whittle, "you better be . . . please, Ali, be on time."

6

MA KEEPS THE ENGINE RUNNING AFTER WE PARK THE NEXT afternoon. Heat blasts from the vents. The wipers arc. In front of us, Como Park slews with freezing rain. There are no picnicking families. No jogging dog walkers like we'd see each time we came here this fall.

"You sure you want to walk?" she asks, but instead of responding, I open the door. She yells, "It's getting shitty out there."

Ma stands by the door to make sure I get up OK, then closes it as I cane-click across the concrete. The park is soft and undone.

I over-the-shoulder glance—next to the car, Ma is staring up into freezing rain with her eyes closed— then take a deep breath and flip my cane into the air and stumble into the sleety grass. I stagger and stomp away from the parking lot, the atrophied muscles in my legs working, just barely, by themselves. Black-trunked trees trapeze around me. Icy rain raps down. I laugh and churn and start to run.

Behind me, I hear Ma yelling, "Ali, what the fuck are you doing?"

When the vertigo pulls me down I'm gasping for air. It's more exercise than I've gotten in months. Gassed, I roll to my back and watch the gray-sheeted sky. I'm soaked and laughing when Ma kneels and frisks her hands over me.

"Are you OK? You OK?" Her face is wet with drizzle. She grabs me hard, holding a balled fist of my jacket for a moment before caressing my chin. "What the fuck?" she says softly. "Come on, Ali. You need to be careful."

"Holy shit!" I smile. "Ma, did you see me go?"

She sits in the freezing grass, propping herself against my side. After a minute, we smile at each other and laugh. We laugh ourselves empty. And then, the park quiets except for our breathing. Snow begins falling and Ma starts to cry.

"I think I'm done walking for the day," I laugh again.

"Doesn't matter," she says, grinning through her tears. She hugs me. "You're fucking grounded anyway."

Ma holds me and our breath unfolds around us.

"Hey, Ma?"

"'S'up, Ali?"

"Ma, I'm really fucking sad, you know?"

"Yeah, I know you are, Ali. You know that's fine,

right?" She tugs at my cheeks and our coats thicken with snow. "It's all right to be sad, Ali," she says, kissing my face. "It's normal." Around us, snow writes through the air, blooming with Ma's voice—"It's all right, Ali. It's all right."

THE CAR IS LEADEN WITH SILENCE DURING THE DRIVE HOME. Storefronts broom by, grainy and slow. Blurred by the falling snow, they look hundreds of miles away.

"Oh, Ali," Ma says, parking on Osceola, "it's really wonderful watching you—"

"Ma, I was thinking . . . It's time to start talking about how I'm going to live on my own. Don't you think?"

She doesn't say anything so I tell her that I'm going to find an apartment and ask my father for money to live off. I might try to get a job. I will go back to school in a year. Casey and Lars will take me to rehab and checkups.

"How are you going to take care of yourself?" She turns the wipers off, but the snow melts as soon as it touches the glass.

"I can do it. It'll happen."

"What are you going to do next year without all of your friends?"

"Shit," I laugh grimly. "Guess I'm going to be a veteran." I tap the window with my cane. "It's gonna suck." The house is dark except for the kitchen light she always leaves on.

Happy

Ma begins to lecture me—*What about all the things you need to do? What about groceries and cooking? Who's going to make sure you're doing what you're supposed to be doing? What happens if you need something? What if you fall down?*

"Al? What about that stuff?"

"I'll figure it out, Ma."

"Don't you think we should wait a bit longer?"

We sit for a long time and snow frosts the windshield. In the same instant that I tell Ma it's probably a good idea if she goes back to Oklahoma, I realize that I've forgotten about her birthday.

"Another month?"

"Ma, I love you, but I need to do this." I stare away from her so she doesn't see my face. "I *have* to do this."

"Couple of weeks?" Her voice gets soft and she shuts the car off.

"I love you tons, Ma, but I think you can go." It starts to get cold as snow insulates us and I can barely hear her.

"Ali?"

"Ma, you gotta."

XI

March 2004

I KNOCK AGAINST THE FROSTED CAR WINDOW. AND FINALLY. after a minute of pounding. Ma rolls toward the glass and wakes. She blinks sleepily, then grins and swings the door open.

"What do you want, mister?" she groans dazedly. "Too early, man!"

"Ma! What are you doing? Why didn't you ring the buzzer?"

"Why you bugging me, Ali?" she laughs. "I need my beauty rest."

"Why didn't you knock? Come up?"

"What makes you think I'm here to see you? Ha! Oooooh, gotcha! Good morning, Al!" Her face is a mask of sleep lines. Below her blizzard of hair, she's wearing a white jean jacket and a red winter coat.

"Ma, why didn't you wake me up when you got here? You knew I was home."

"Ali!" She stretches next to the car, sings, "Good morning, good morning!"

"Ma, you should have knocked. There's a futon in the attic."

"Didn't want to bother you." She says that she was fine, that she's only been here a couple of hours. "But hey, Al! I'm glad you're up! 'Bout time, sonny boy!"

"Ma. You should have come up."

"Shit, don't worry about me so much." She laughs. "You're the baby, the tiny one. I'm the Ma! You let me fret."

"Ma."

She sits back in the car, ignoring me, and rubs her face.

I'd forgotten that she was visiting.

She grins and acts delirious—looks up and out of the corners of her eyes, trying to look innocent—then grabs a brush from the cup holder.

"Ma. You should have—"

"You see a hair tie around here?" she asks, rooting through the books in the passenger seat. "Can't find shit in here. Look what I got." She peels a piece of taped paper off the dash and hands it to me. It's a quote from Voltaire—*Paradise is where I am.*

"What do you think of that?" She says, "Yep," and nods a series of exclamation marks. For years I'd teased her about the books and calendars of daily affirmations we had lying around our homes, the self-fulfilling prophecy and mantra tapes she listened to in her bedroom.

"Already knew it." I read the Voltaire again and smile. Each couple of months, she mails me a new lovingkindness or meditation book. She doesn't think I read them but I do. I always have.

"So, Ali, what do you want to do today? Whatever you want, we'll do it." Standing in the morning light, she smiles and brushes her hair. "HI-YA!" she shouts, and bangs the comb into the car when she's done.

"Ma, I want to get *this* tattooed on my back." I hand back the line from Voltaire. "What do *you* think of that? You want to get it too? That's what I want to do. Let's do it."

"Oh Lordy." She shakes her head and laughs. "You and your ink. Going to run out of room or get blood poisoning. How 'bout next time? I gotta build shelves for your records. Brought the saw." She points to the back of the car and then pinches my side. "Some poetry books back there, too, Ali! Hey, by the way, I love you, Tiny." She says it again and I can't stop smiling. "I love you, Tinacious! You know, you're looking pretty good! I love the shaved head." She scruffs a palm over my scalp, then squeezes a skin-roll on the back of my neck until I wince.

I haven't planned anything. I'd forgotten about her and she slept in her car.

"You get the John Hammond CD I sent?" she asks, popping the hatchback. "Got some good stuff for you."

I tell her that I listen to it every day, and she grins,

then asks if I want to go to the really garlicky place for breakfast.

"Yeah, Ma. Coffee News sounds great. But is that what you want to do?"

"Is that what *you* want? Shit, let's compromise. You decide what we're gonna do, and then, how 'bout you pay? That sounds like a plan."

"OK, Ma. Perfect." I smile but there's a knot in my throat; I don't want to stop hugging her. "I'm so glad you're here, Ma. I love *you*, you know that?"

"Yeah, well, you need to read more books so you can beat me at Scrabble, *and* you need to get more sleep. *Buuuuut*, sorry to say, Ali, you'll still lose." She pinches my face delightedly. "Listen to your Ma, Al! Oh, and right back at ya. I love you too, Al." She beams. "Big time."

I rest my cheek on the top of her head while she hugs me, and for the first time in my life I can feel what her words mean. The tightness, the just-bearable despair in my chest thaws, melts, breaks apart. Light courses through my veins. I can feel the world pin-balling around me. With Ma right next to me, I do not want to die. I close my eyes and listen to us breathe and let myself cry deeply.

Ma tugs my cheeks again, then pushes away and hops back and claps and moonwalks across the street.

Epilogue

2008

WHEN I MERGE ONTO I-25 SOUTH, THE SKY IS AN OBSIDIAN bowl above Pueblo, Colorado—and my fiancée's sleepy warmth is still suffusing the car air. Minutes ago, she handed my road-trip food through the window and kissed me good-bye. Curled in a pink sweater, squinting into the headlights, she waved from the driveway.

The nystagmus and double vision have gotten so bad that I drive hunched over the wheel with one eye closed. And it's not just my eyesight—for the past eight years, all of my disabilities have worsened. By the end of 2005, my second year as an English professor at Macalester College, I was avoiding my students' writing. I could barely read. The vertigo's never gone away, and I fell down again and again. The fall of 2006 I

283

took a medical leave and started wearing an eye patch again.

There are days I can't read, days my face, my body go numb, and a couple of times each year I rush to the nearest hospital for an MRI and a new battery of tests. But after a decade of living with a black hole inside me, three years ago, I tossed out all of my drugs and booze. I realized I've always had a bottomless reservoir of love and learned to love without doing anything at all.

Almost daily, that little boy in the dark room comes to me. And welcoming him is the hardest thing I do, the hardest thing I'll ever do. Kneeling in front of myself, no matter how many times I falter and have to start over, I tell him that I will take care of him. That he's wonderful. Holding him, I tell him that I love him.

With the car windows down, the freeway is a rush of darkness beside me. The Colorado air is cold and dry and the road is empty. If I make good time I'll get to Ma's house in New Mexico at two this afternoon.

Still, there are nights, after trying my best all day, when the darkness is stifling. When my depression and anger claw at me, I sit in my room with everything off. Silence washes over me and I let myself feel my sadness and rage. I embrace them. Eventually, I call my friends and tell them that I'm having a bad day, that I love them. I walk or jog along River Road, where Ma used to push my wheelchair. At least once a day, I reread the e-mail Ma sent me when I asked her how I got my real name.

Happy

If I remember right—

Sam or Alex were the options I think when you were born like within minutes I asked your father "Sam or Alex?" and he said Alex. I think that's the way it was. The girl's name I was thinking was "Emma Rose Ann" after Emma Goldman the anarchist. Rose, flower. For a boy I wanted a name that was a ROCK. Like a MANLY name if you were a boy. And nickname was good too. AL. And Alex meant a good thing too: defender of men. When people are pregnant they are always checking out books to find the significance of names. Can't remember what Sam meant, though. Maybe your father has a different spin on that one. I think it's right, though.

Love, yer Ma

As the car speeds up Raton Pass, sunlight outlines the mountain tips to the east, casting alternating lines over the interstate. When the road flattens out, for hundreds of miles around me, the morning is bright and empty. Because Casey won't be up until noon, I leave a message on his cell. Holding my phone out of the window, I scream, "Rise and shine, motherfucker!" And then, even though he'll chuckle and ask me why I'm getting all soft, I tell him that I love him.

٭ ٭ ٭

HITCHHIKERS HUG THE HIGHWAYS NORTH OF GALLUP THAT afternoon. It's almost a hundred degrees, and they walk backward in long-sleeve shirts and dark pants, thumbs curved up, gleaming like metal. Empty plastic bags blow across the cracked concrete. Litter fills the ditches' dead grass. What I think is a heap of rags on the shoulder, heat waves shimmering up from the pile, is, when I zoom by, a sunburned man.

Rock formations cover the landscape—boulders are stacked on fragile spires of worn-down stone.

When I drive over the cow-grate on the outskirts of town, the glove box pops open and the Wolf Parade CD I'm listening to skips. The rumble reminds me to breathe and I tug at my numb face. Rolling the window down, I let the hot wind fill my mouth.

It feels like there's a beehive in my chest and it is on fire and beautiful and it is there always and forever and I start to weep I'm so happy.

On the distant horizon, somewhere over Arizona, rain clouds crouch, gathering. A rope of smoke climbs from the red bluffs and I smell burning piñon. I slow the overheating car but still bang through the potholes, past the shotgunned sign covered in graffiti. A pack of feral dogs bark alongside me as I turn onto Ma's street.

BOB'S STRAW HAT SHADES HIS ENTIRE TORSO; HE SITS IN A chair on the shoulder of the road, angling a palette knife and adjusting his oil painting. The sun is just rising over the bluffs, but already, heat waves undulate up from the barren field he's facing. The pavement sticks to my shoes as I jog up the road behind him.

"How's it going, Al?" he asks without looking from the canvas.

I cough out a "Good" and say it's getting too hot. He's barely audible in the morning wind, asking if I'm wearing sunscreen. When I glance back, he's tilted toward the easel, daubing, then looking up to study the red-gold hills.

The whine of the bike chain gets louder than my breath, and suddenly, Ma is coasting next to me. "Go, Tiny," she shouts, pedaling hard, passing me on the incline. "Go go go go!"

I pick up the wooden stake that I dropped yesterday and then race to catch up, yelling that mutts have been attacking me when I get to the driveway ahead of us. "Mean little fuckers, Ma," I shout. "Watch out!"

Near the hilltop, she asks again about my failing eyesight even though we talked about it earlier this week. "Why exercise if it makes you feel worse?" she huffs.

"Want me to sit in my room, peeking out the window?" I laugh, but I'm heavy breathing. "It makes me feel awake. Muscles, all thrilled. Everything"—I gasp and cough—"feels right. Possible." I slow because my thighs are spazzing and she cruises by, not saying anything. "Know what I mean, Ma?"

"But you're going to get your checkup, right? *You are*," she says over her shoulder. "You'll call and set up an appointment today. Get an MRI. The usual? You gotta do it. Do it for your Ma."

"Already left the doctor a message, and I'll call again when we get home," I shout. "Promise, promise, promise."

At the crest, she sees me getting close and bears down on the pedals. Racing down the blacktop, her hair hovers behind her like a white shawl. She keeps looking back and yelling, but I can't hear her.

Cheeks flushed, Ma waits by the stop sign at the bottom of the road. "You're slow," she grins, teasing me while I stretch and gulp air. "Come on, Tiny. We're all going to die, but not yet! Not today! Where you at?"

When Ma sidles off the bike and stares out at Red Lake, I start sprinting back up the hill.

For ten minutes there's only the wind in my face, a heartbeat in my ears. And then, Ma's shouting my name and I hear the bike behind me. When I slow, she pulls beside me, pedaling smoothly, pacing me. "Come on, Al," she cheers. "No problem, Ali! Come on."

Over the ochre butte a blackbird wheels in the sky.

"I know you don't want to hear what I'm about to say," she says, starting one of her lectures. "But—"

"Ma, come on." I stare at the road's painted line. The pavement glitters. "Shit, I'm trying to work out here."

"What I was *going* to say, Al"—she sighs theatrically—"if you'd let me talk for once. You're not that fast!" she laughs. "But you're good, Ali. You're a good man."

Happy

Ma turns to me and smiles and my blood gathers and swells.

We labor up the sweltering incline without speaking. I smile, tears mixing with the sweat. I'm openmouthed and gasping, but I speed up to stay next to her. Over the lilting clop of my strides, Ma shifts gears and sings into the endless light.

Big Love

To my brilliant & big-hearted editor, Alexis Gargagliano, & the rest of the wonderful Scribner folks; my agent, Amy Williams, for believing in me & this book when it was gibberish; & all of the people who've helped me along the way—Dr. Doom, Dr. Samuel Thomas, Wendy Whelihan, Suzanne Rivecca, Kathleen Glasgow, Ray Gonzalez, Nate Slawson, Craig & Brenda & Cal, Dr. Tenenbaum, Ada Limon, Polly Carden, Jess Grover & Adam Clay.

To my family & friends, I give you all of my love, all of my everything—especially Ma & Bob, Simone, Dad & Lindy, Casey & Jihan, Adam, Amos, Gran, Keenan, Jason, the Harmes Clan, Seth, Erin, Jonny, Brown, Austin, Rhea, Shak, Laurel, Lars, J.M., S.M.P., my colleagues at Macalester College & Texas Christian University, the people at Tin House, Milkweed Editions, &

all of the Fighting Scots. Apologies & love to anyone I've forgotten.

This book, this life, would be nothing without the strength & kindness & unending love of my wife, Dr. Ariane Balizet.

About the Author

ALEX LEMON WAS BORN IN IOWA AND LIVES IN FORT WORTH, Texas. He teaches at Texas Christian University. He is the author of three collections of poetry, *Mosquito* (Tin House Books), *Hallelujah Blackout* (Milkweed Editions), and *Fancy Beasts* (Milkweed Editions), and is the recipient of a fellowship from the National Endowment for the Arts.

A Q&A with Alex Lemon

Q: "Happy" is one of the nicknames you were given in college. How would you describe this persona that you inhabited in college?

A: Happy was/is carefree, casual, and jubilant. Excessive in every facet of a young man's life. Yearning for the good time, what probably seemed to most people who knew me like I was interested in pleasure, getting fucked-up. At the same time, I tried to make everyone else feel good (because I felt so shitty). I was friendly to everyone, and all of the swaggering guy-talk and joking was, like it is for many young men who don't know how to talk about how they feel, the way men I knew showed affection for each other. I hug everyone now but, for whatever reason, "men" didn't do that; we'd call each other douche bag or asshole. Compassion was punching someone in the shoulder. So many people knew who Happy was, but I wore that Happy Mask so well that no one really knew who I was. No one knew what dark emptiness I felt inside me because I was tricking everyone around me. And really, I'd lost myself so completely that I was deluding myself. The more I tried to be Happy, the more I felt like I didn't exist at all. And that's really the emotional key to the entire book, that Happy was this surface character, like a bodysuit, a mask that didn't allow anyone in to see how troubled I was.

Q: Reading this book is an incredibly visceral experience. It opens with you waking up with bouncing vision and an aching body; the whole room is spinning. It's disorienting in a way that puts the reader right inside your body.

A: Good! I did my best to replicate that feeling, that unnerving dislocation that is, at the same time incredibly gut-wrenching. There's such a huge, huge challenge in trying to articulate pain and discomfort because it's so located in only one way in each individual person. And I'd much rather have someone react to my work with deep feelings—love, disgust, disbelief, compassion, amazement, even palpable dislike—than a shoulder shrug.

Q: How would you describe the kind of person you were before your stroke?

A: On the surface, I was trying to be the all-American boy—I did all the things that "real men" are supposed to—played sports, partied, casually hooked up, woke up in strange places, and laughed about it all, etc. But I was much more complicated than that. I was interested in my classes but all of the people around me seemed so smart that I'd tell my best friend, Casey, that I was going to class and then I'd walk around the neighborhood getting high. Later, I'd go back to my room and read. But before my medical issues I felt different. I was already confused and scared because I kept the sexual abuse I suffered as a boy secret from the people around me. And I was also too interested in the arts and all sorts of artistic and intellectual zaniness to fit in perfectly with most of the athletes, and I liked listening to baseball games and lifting weights too much to feel totally accepted in the art studios. I spent more time in the ceramic studio than I did playing baseball in college, but it didn't matter where I was, I was lost.

Q: **Up until your brain surgery you lived an incredibly physical life; what was it like to have to relearn how to navigate the world when you had such a different physical relationship to it?**

A: Imagine being forced to sit motionless when every inch of you itches because, like some end-of-days plague, all of your insides, your organs, even your heart, has athlete's foot.

Think about sprinkling yourself with gasoline and then, as you try to will your hand to stop moving, you have to watch as that hand, that hand that used to be under your control, picks up a match, lights it, and then drops it on your lap. But that fire doesn't end it—there's pain, of course, but even more traumatic is what happens in your mind as you watch the flames without being able to do anything. You watch, powerless, while it all falls apart. The flame never goes out and it never stops hurting and all you can do is think "Whoa! Shit. I'm on fire."

Q: When did you first start writing?

A: I'd always written. I was raised in a world of art and literature and music, and that home life had a tremendous impact on me. I did my best to ignore it, but it was always a part of my core. We didn't have a TV, so I read and scribbled in journals. I wrote in college, kept notebooks, wrote poems, but I thought I was going to be a lawyer because I thought that being rich would somehow make me feel better about myself. I was a couple of art classes away from an art major. I can't remember why now, but I was deathly afraid of art history. I refused to take it. Maybe, because my vision began failing after the bleeds started, that I knew there was no way I could look at slides all day. Or maybe I was just scared and it was easier to follow what seemed like a very clear path to my major in poli-sci.

I didn't start taking writing seriously until two of my professors at Macalester College, the wonderful writers Wang Ping and Diane Glancy, told me that writing and studying literature was something that I should consider doing. This happened after I returned to Mac after taking a year off to recover from the brain surgery. It was an incredibly powerful moment for me. I was so depressed and manic and self-destructive. To hear someone I respect say that they thought I was a talented writer was more healing than any medicine or drug I've taken. Sometime in the year after my surgery, I started going to Casey's writing class. Ping watched me hobble noisily into class—at the time I was using a cane, banging it into everything around me and wearing an eye patch—and she asked me straight up what had happened. She didn't treat me like I was pitiable or a freak or a monster; she treated me like I was normal. Ping let me attend the class as often as I wanted. Writing was and is hard and complicated and it's sometimes painful or emotional, but it has always filled me with pleasure. In hindsight I can see how I've always been drawn to those attributes—complexity, challenge, beauty, a bit of pain, and deep feeling—but however excruciating writing was, it wasn't self-destructive and it didn't hurt the people around me.

Q: Did it offer some solace?
A: No. But that wasn't the point for me, so I wasn't

seeking it out. It was more about acknowledging the actual. The real. That varying degrees of suffering and pain are as much a part of life as breathing and that no matter what sort of trash or wreckage one is digging through, if you look close enough, you can see that we're always surrounded by a tremendous beauty. Oh, man—does that sound cheesy? Shitbags. Balls. There, I feel better. But seriously, *Happy* is more than a story about medical trauma or addiction. It's about masculinity and mental illness; and in the end, the book is a love story about a mother and son.

Q: Do you think you would have become a writer if you'd never had any physical problems?

A: I think, no matter how I made my living, I would have written, but that's very different from becoming a writer. I don't really know. What has happened in my life has become such a part of me; I've learned to acknowledge it all, to confront, tend to my feelings about everything that's happened, etc., to such a degree that I can't imagine that what-if.

Q: You've published several books of poetry. How was the switch to prose?

A: In the beginning it was incredibly difficult. Though I'd always read a lot of prose, I'd spent the years leading up to the writing of *Happy* fully immersed in poetry. So instead of using the precision and focus I used when writing verse to write crisp, clear, vibrant pages of prose, at the start of this project, I was writing a four-hundred-page hyperlyrical and endlessly confusing poem. But I practiced, and like almost everything, the more time I spent writing prose, the more that poetry skill set began smoothly transferring to my prose. And with it came a similar pleasure to that which comes to me when I write poetry. In the end it was wonderful.

Q: You've been sober for several years. The book doesn't really cover that period of your life. What made you finally want to get sober? When was that? Why do you think it took you so long?

A: I was literally destroying myself. I was never using for fun or to have a good time. I was trying to obliterate myself so I wouldn't think about all those parts of me that spun me into the darkness, all those difficulties that I've had to deal with and face and confront. I started trying to get my shit together halfway through graduate school. I failed, repeatedly failed, and so every few months I'd declare a "Human Experiment" that entailed getting as fucked-up as possible and staying that way for as long as I could. Everyone was a winner! At the time, it seemed like a perfectly reasonable way to dive back into the darkness. I'm not sure why it took so long. Wait, that's a lie. I do know why it took so long. But first, why don't mammals come out of the womb fully formed?

Q: This book doesn't have the traditional tidy, happy ending. What is your health like now?

A: I didn't want to write that kind of book, and wrap it up with a tidy little bow, because that, to me, seems so incredibly dishonest. A willful ignoring of reality in every way. So much of life is not tidy. To varying degrees, suffering and pain are as much a part of our lives as breathing air. And if one pays attention and really sees all of the messiness, so much of our ugly wrecks, are, yeah, maybe a little ugly, but if you tilt your head or squint just so, or open your eyes wide, they are also tremendously beautiful.

As for my health, I guess there are good days and bad days. I live with visual disabilities—nystagmus and diplopia—and some days you might catch me wearing my eye patch or a black contact that occludes my vision in that eye. I still have some numbness in my face, and sometimes in my hands. My gait has improved but it's still off. I fall to my right. And I can be really awkward. I bumble into corners and knock into walls. If you're walking beside me, I'll knock into you because my steps angle forward and out to make sure I don't tip. I'm a jagged walker. I also have some chronic pain in my back and legs. And all of my symptoms get worse if I'm tired or stressed out, and I still have to spend time visiting neurologists and neuropthalmologists and every few months I feel like the world is ending and I'll go get an MRI. For the most part, I've learned to deal with the vicissitudes of my health. I know what makes me feel good and I know what will make me feel worse. I have learned to do most of the things I want to do while still taking care of myself.

Q: The book isn't exactly filled with happy romantic relationships, but you're married now?

A: I am and I couldn't be more thrilled about it. We have a household filled with love and books and good music and one cat named Catface. I'm very fortunate: I get to share my life with a brilliant and beautiful woman whom I've known for years. She was amazingly supportive while I worked on *Happy*. She's an incredible reader and understood why I felt like denigrating or judging many of the college men in the book was, in many ways, erasing their humanness or denying their feelings. And as a scholar, she knows about literature's machinations. So she was there. She was present, emotionally and intellectually. And so we've gotten older and our love has grown and grown because I am and have been there for her, totally and completely. It's good stuff.

Q: What are you working on next?

A: Right now I'm working really hard on not hitting my head on things. I have a long history of head trauma and it's about time that I put an end to it. I should probably wear a giant foam helmet at all times. As for my writing: I'm working on three projects. The first is a book of prose that picks up where *Happy* ends: a young man both broken and healed. I'm still very interested in some ideas that were brought up in *Happy*, like constructs of masculinity, ability/disability, and mental illness, but I'm also thinking more broadly about the idea of fatherhood and the pleasures of the physical body. I'm also at work on my fourth collection of poetry (the third collection, *Fancy Beasts*, was published by Milkweed Editions in 2009). This new collection is a sequence of poems in dialogue with Emerson's "Beauty." Finally, I'm gathering/organizing my essays into a book that I'm calling *Rabbit-Hole Music*.

Printed in the United States
By Bookmasters